DAYS
(I'LL REMEMBER ALL MY LIFE)

KELVIN BARKER

Days (I'll Remember All My Life)

ISBN: 9798824401059

Typesetting and design: Mark Worrall
Photographs: Kelvin Barker
www.gate17books.co.uk

CONTENTS

ACKNOWLEDGEMENTS

I am indebted to everybody who gets a mention in this book, each one of them has played their part in my own personal history to date (even the copper who arrested me in Portsmouth). They are all too many to include on one page, but hopefully they will enjoy reading about themselves as they flick through the following pages. Those who I have mentioned but will never be able to read what I said, God bless you. You will be forever missed, but thank you for coming into my life and enriching it, albeit too briefly.

Thanks, as ever, go to my immediate and wider family, but especially my wife and my world, Lisa, and my children Daniel, Poppy and Sam. And not forgetting Charlotte and my beautiful grandson Jacob.

I've dedicated this book to my parents, John and Noreen. As I write this, John remains at the head of the family, and still gets to hear my anguished rants about Chelsea every few days. He doesn't rant the way I do, but he still shares my anguish. Sadly, he lives alone now as Noreen resides in a care home as she fights the unwinnable fight against dementia. I miss the old Mum, but still love the current version all the same. These *Days (I'll Remember All My Life)* are all thanks to them.

Finally, as always, I'm so grateful to Mark Worrall for all the advice and assistance he has given me in getting this book written and published. He's a good bloke and a good friend.

This book is dedicated with love and thanks to my mum and dad,
John and Noreen xx.

INTRODUCTION

It was during the great pandemic lockdown of 2020 that a thought occurred to me. Lying idly in the hot afternoon sun, with no particular place to go, my thoughts turned as they so often do to football. Later that year, on Saturday 5th December to be precise, it would be the 50th anniversary of my first visit to Stamford Bridge. The first professional football match I had attended. The first time I had clapped eyes on Chelsea Football Club in the flesh. And it was love at first sight.

Fifty years is a long time and my particular half-century of Chelsea worship has seen me take in a good few thousand football matches, with many more thousands of memories accumulated. Somehow or other, almost all my major life events have a football memory attached. To be honest, the same can be said of the majority of my minor life events. Perhaps this is no surprise; after all, despite a few vague black and white recollections of rainy walks in a push-chair and kaleidoscopically-bright late-60s toddler birthday parties with equally small friends and, more importantly, cakes as big as the party-goers, my first really clear memory is of the day I made my Stamford Bridge bow. I remember the huge crowds and feeling, perhaps like any diminutive five-year-old would, completely intimidated by them. I remember hearing words I'd never heard before. You know the ones. I heard loads of them. I remember the general din both inside and outside the ground, because it was even louder than the Slade records my dad was playing at the time. And I felt dwarfed by the enormous floodlight pylons which stood tall at all four corners of the ground. But most of all, I remember the Blues won 1-0 courtesy of a Keith Weller wondergoal, and that from that moment onwards I was always going to be Chelsea.

The title of this book is a nod to a fantastic song by one of my favourite bands, The Kinks. When one of my childhood heroes, Ray Wilkins, sadly passed away in April 2018, I put a link to this song on my social media with a picture of our former skipper as a simple tribute to a Chelsea great. The words seemed fitting in the same way that the title fits this book. Be the memories good, bad, happy, sad or just downright random, what is inside these pages are reflections on days I'll remember all my life, and how they link to Chelsea Football Club. Of course, The Kinks are famously led by the Davies brothers, Ray and Dave, who are keen Arsenal supporters. However, to prove I can generally find a meaningful link where one is needed, The Kinks are a band which had a strong influence on Madness, who have always held a place in the hearts of Chelsea supporters of my age, not only for the part they played musically during our adolescent years, but also because in lead singer Suggs and drummer Woody, they included members who were Chelsea terrace stalwarts. Later they would feature a friend of mine, Graham Bush, on bass for four years. Graham is also a lifelong Chelsea supporter and season ticket holder to this day.

So, let's start right at the very beginning. I was born in a house, number two Carthew Villas, just off the iconic Goldhawk Road and within yards of where Hammersmith meets Shepherds Bush. If you walk past that house now, there is evidence that I lived there. This book. The only blue plaque I have is something I've discussed with my dentist.

My local team was Queens Park Rangers, so obviously supporting my local team was out of the question. I had my whole life ahead of me, why would I actively encourage humiliation throughout it? Fortunately, my dad supported another team, Chelsea, so that was me sorted. Had my dad supported QPR, my name would be Nigel and I would still be waiting for my first sexual encounter. My parents called me Kelvin, which isn't ideal, but I think it's an upgrade on Nigel the virginal super hoop.

I had the misfortune of living and growing up in Shepherds Bush throughout the 1970s and early-80s, a period during which QPR were regularly a better team than Chelsea. That was nice at school. Most of my friends supported the R's and I had to regularly take their teasing on the chin. My best retort after a defeat at Loftus Road was to remind them that their fans had been caught hiding in dustbins after the game, but when you're a nine-year-old primary school pupil, it's probably not entirely appropriate to be taunting your friends about football hooliganism. They did famously hide in dustbins though, after an evening game in 1975.

Of course, as parsimonious as my early Chelsea-supporting years were in terms of success, the second half of my 50-year term has been a consistent stream of glorious achievement for the mighty Blues. In simple terms: we've won everything that's worth winning. And I'm fortunate enough to have witnessed all of it. But this book isn't about the glory of supporting the modern-day Chelsea, or gloating about the triumphs. They get a mention, of course. But this is about the day-to-day stuff, and how supporting Chelsea has linked in with it. The friendships and the friends, including some we've lost along the way. Heroes and villains. Villains who became heroes. Heroes who became villains. Heroes who became friends. The family ties. The tears that preceded the numerous smiles of recent success. The school playground and workplace banter. Births, deaths and marriages, all wrapped up in blue. I hope you enjoy reading it as much as I enjoyed writing it.

Come on you mighty Blues!

SATURDAY 3RD FEBRUARY 1973

FA Cup Round Four
Chelsea 2 Ipswich Town 0

Ipswich Town, under the trusty stewardship of Bobby Robson, were a club which was going places. By the end of the 1970s they would have won an FA Cup, and were at the beginning of a period in which they really should have added a League title. They did build on their FA Cup success with a UEFA Cup triumph in 1981, but it all went south for the Suffolk club after Robson left to take over as manager of England a year later. For me, I had already accrued a happy memory of playing against them when, over Christmas 1971, defender David Webb had famously played an entire ninety minutes in goal against them and kept a clean sheet in a 2-0 victory. I had been there with my dad and brother, and we had all witnessed Chelsea's cockney tough guy run onto the pitch wearing the green number one shirt and, in front of the supporters in the Shed, drop to his knees and offer a prayer to the Lord. Classic Webby – what a character.

On the occasion of the FA Cup game in February 1973, it is probably fair to say that logistics had gone out of the window. My dad used to drive us to games but when I got older, I would often do the journey on foot. It took about an hour but we did live, literally, within walking distance of Stamford Bridge. However, for reasons I have long since forgotten, on the weekend of the 1973 FA Cup fourth round we would be staying with my aunt, uncle and cousins in Basingstoke. Not to be deterred, though, we would still be at the Bridge for the big game. My dad, my Uncle Pete, my cousin Steven, my brother Keith and me. Keith and I always loved seeing Steven, so we knew it was going to be a good day.

There was an old tradition back in the FA Cup's heyday, whereby clubs would often wear either their away strip for home ties or perhaps an entirely different kit altogether from their normal strip. I distinctly recall an FA Cup clash in the early-1970s between Derby County and Leeds United during which the Rams wore an all blue kit, and the Peacocks wore all red. Neither side were in their traditional white. Of course, Nike and Chelsea announced a new kit to be worn during the 2019/20 FA Cup campaign, which took inspiration from the Blues' first ever triumph in the competition, fifty years earlier. Naturally enough, though, in these cynical and more commercially-aware times, it proved to be nothing more than a marketing opportunity and the very smart new kit, which sold in huge numbers, was worn just once during Chelsea's run to the Wembley final. But I digress.

We drove from Basingstoke to SW6 on the morning of the game, Steven, Keith and I giggling inanely throughout the journey while the adults behaved, well, like adults. When we got to the Bridge, we took our places on the North Stand terrace, the three of us kids going right down to the front and situating ourselves directly behind the goal that Ipswich would be defending in the first half. We spotted that *The Big Match* cameras were there, which only added to the excitement, as TV coverage was minimal back then when compared to the blanket coverage of the modern day.

The teams ran out, both wearing their away strips. Chelsea, dressed in their Hungarian 'Magnificent Magyars'-inspired kit of red shirts, white shorts and green socks (or stockings, as Brian Moore no doubt referred to them in commentary) were up against an Ipswich side in yellow and blue. After a cagey start, the deadlock was broken just after the half-hour mark when burly, aggressive striker Bill Garner, probably not a native of Budapest, channelled his inner Puskas with a lovely lob over the onrushing visitors' 'keeper, David Best. Perhaps his middle name was Second? That the goal had been scored directly in front of Steven, Keith and I just made it all the more exciting.

Having formally changed his name at half-time, Ferenc Garner doubled his and Chelsea's tally immediately after the break, with a goal at the opposite end of the ground which Steven, Keith and I celebrated as if we had actually seen it go in. It was the final goal of a surprisingly routine victory for the Blues, who would go into the hat for the fifth round, whilst the five of us would go into the car for the journey back to Basingstoke.

Now, it's important at this point to note the proximity of Stamford Bridge from our home, and compare it to the proximity of Stamford Bridge from Basingstoke. Because on the journey back – and you probably don't need to be Miss Marple to work out the next bit – my dad's car broke down. We were stuck at the roadside for hours, waiting in the freezing cold for somebody from the AA to arrive. Steven, Keith and I initially thought it was all very amusing, but when we started laughing at the AA man when he finally arrived, we received the ticking off we probably deserved.

Needless to say, it was approaching midnight before our car

chuntered into the driveway of Uncle Pete's house. Whatever the reason for the visit to Basingstoke, if it included a Saturday night on the tiles, those plans were held in abeyance. But there was some good news on the horizon. Before we left for home the following day, we all watched *The Big Match* together. And as big Bill Garner lobbed the goalkeeper to give Chelsea the lead, there on the screen were Steven, Keith and I, cheering wildly as the ball hit the back of the net.

SATURDAY 1ST JANUARY 1977

Football League Division Two

Chelsea 5 Hereford United 1

Despite winning major trophies in the first two years of the 1970s, Chelsea became cash-strapped and relegated by the middle of the decade. One of the most fashionable clubs in the country, at the turn of the 70s it seemed Chelsea were well placed to push on and become a major force both at home and on the continent. The Blues' only league title to date had been won 15 years earlier, but another was a distinct possibility before a catastrophic malaise set in against the backdrop of over-ambitious redevelopment plans, a harsh economic decline, and difficult relationships between manager Dave Sexton and a number of his best players. Relegation came in 1975, by which time loyal and tough Scottish defender Eddie McCreadie had taken on the manager's role.

With most of the players who had taken Sexton's team to the brink of greatness now plying their trade elsewhere, and money for replacements scant, McCreadie had no option but to blood a number of youngsters who had risen through the ranks of the Chelsea schoolboy and youth teams. Ray Wilkins, given the captaincy by McCreadie while he was still in his teens, was the shining light of a squad which included fellow youth products such as Steve Finnieston, Gary Stanley, Teddy Maybank, Tommy Langley, Steve Wicks, Ray Lewington, John Sparrow and Graham Wilkins, elder brother of Ray. Ian Britton, Micky Droy and Gary Locke provided a little more experience and were slightly older than the aforementioned players, while David Hay had joined from Celtic in the summer of 1974, following an outstanding showing for Scotland in the World Cup held in West Germany that year. Peter Bonetti, John Dempsey and Ron Harris remained at the Bridge and were genuine links to the heyday of Sexton's Chelsea, as was Charlie Cooke, who had returned from a stint with Crystal Palace. Ian Hutchinson remained with the club but was rarely fit, and Ferenc Garner was also still on the books but, like Hutchinson, struggled with injuries as a result of his brave endeavours and willingness to put his body in harm's way.

Reputations counted for nothing during the Blues' first year in Division Two and they finished the season in 11th place, slap bang in the middle of the table. A run to the fifth round of the FA Cup gave some cause for optimism, before a demoralising defeat at home to Third

Division Crystal Palace in front of more than fifty thousand spectators ended that particular route to glory. But there was no more inglorious defeat that season than the one inflicted by Oldham Athletic, who on their first visit to Stamford Bridge in 45 years, and with only one away win in their last 33 games, ran riot in SW6 with a thumping 3-0 victory. McCreadie's task of taking his side back into the top-flight looked a damn sight harder at the end of the 1975/76 season than it had a year earlier, following relegation.

In typically unpredictable style, then, Chelsea's young team suddenly gelled from the start of the following season. They hit the top of the table at the end of September and were still there as 1976 drew to a close. During that time, they'd had another visit from Oldham and had, again, conceded three goals to The Latics. On this occasion, however, the Blues scored four of their own.

By now, we were living in a house in Tadmor Street, Shepherds Bush, which we shared with my grandparents. If this sounds a bit like Charlie and the Chocolate Factory, I will caveat that we didn't all sleep in one bed. I have, though, got a few mates who look like Oompa Loompas.

Chelsea's first game of 1977 was against struggling Hereford United at the Bridge. The night before, as was tradition, my grandparents had thrown a party, and everybody was in good spirits. The following day's game against Hereford was an enjoyable canter on a ploughed field of a pitch, during which Ray Wilkins still managed to score one of the finest goals of the period when he punished a poor goal kick by depositing the ball over the hapless 'keeper's head and into his net. The Blues won 5-1, their top place billing cemented for a couple more weeks.

The following Saturday, Chelsea began their latest quest for FA Cup glory at The Dell, home of holders Southampton, the Division Two side who had shocked mighty Manchester United the previous May to take the cup back with them to Hampshire. The Saints sat 13 points and 15 places below the Blues in Division Two, and when the two had met at the Bridge in October, Chelsea had won 3-1 and put on a display which visiting manager Lawrie McMenemy announced was one of the best he had ever seen in the division.

With away journeys still some distance off for this 11-year-old kid, at the same time as Chelsea were doing battle on the south coast, my dad and I had gone to see QPR play Shrewsbury Town, also in the FA Cup. Walking home, we heard that Chelsea had drawn 1-1 at The Dell and my dad said we would go to the replay on Wednesday. That was something to look forward to as there was no doubt in my mind Chelsea would win and go on to lift the trophy in May. As we reached home, my dad put the key in the door and one of our neighbours was standing on the landing. There was an eerie atmosphere and it was clear that something was wrong. Our neighbour told my dad that my grandad had passed away suddenly that afternoon, having suffered a massive heart attack. The following Monday, arrangements were made for my grandad to be buried in Fulham Cemetery on Thursday – a sure sign of how different the world was in 1977. I knew I wouldn't be going to the FA Cup replay and I understood why. On the Wednesday night at around 10pm, I switched the radio on while I was in bed and heard the news that Southampton had beaten Chelsea 3-0. I switched the radio back off and carried on crying. Happy New Year.

SATURDAY 14TH MAY 1977

Football League Division Two
Chelsea 4 Hull City 0

Eddie McCreadie and his young charges did indeed see the job through, and promotion was confirmed at Molineux, home of Wolverhampton Wanderers, on the penultimate weekend of the season. A draw on that day was probably inevitable, given that the already-promoted home side needed one point to clinch top spot and the title, while the Blues needed a solitary point to confirm their return to Division One. Despite a little wobble after Easter, McCreadie had steadied the ship again for the final run-in, and the last game of the season, at home to Hull City, would now be a ninety minute party. At least that's what everybody thought. In the event, the party was much more enjoyable, far more chaotic and was dragged out over many more than ninety minutes, as Stamford Bridge finally had something to celebrate again.

McCreadie, ever the flamboyant showman, and much loved by the Chelsea supporters, announced that before the game with The Tigers, he would introduce onto the pitch, each member of his squad. Supporters were implored to get in early to witness the celebration of these genuine heroes, most of whom had voluntarily taken a pay cut during the season to help with the club's fight against increasing debt. The fans listened, and Stamford Bridge was full very early. We were standing on the North Stand terrace for this game, on the wraparound with the West Stand. There were flimsy fences erected at either end of the ground, to deter any pitch invaders. It was only when the pitch invasions began that the flimsiness of the fences became apparent.

McCreadie introduced his players one by one, and each was given a much-deserved rousing reception. Once the players had all taken their individual applause, they embarked on a lap of honour which began with twenty or so people in their full kits and tracksuit tops, and ended with a good few hundred more joining them from the terraces. One guy went on from the terraces, joined the lap of honour, and then watched the entire game sitting amongst the photographers behind the North Stand goal. Chelsea supporters' reputation at that time was such that the photographers probably thought it wise to just leave him be.

Once the game belatedly kicked off, there was a carnival atmosphere inside the ground. Steve Finnieston, enjoying the best goal scoring season of his career, found the net to give Chelsea a half-time lead. However, that goal was met with another pitch invasion, pushing back the end time of the match even further.

After the players emerged for the second half, a young skinhead came racing onto the pitch with a bunch of flowers in his hands. As the teams were lining up for the kick-off, the young lad headed straight to Ray Wilkins, handed him the flowers, dropped to his knees and kissed the Chelsea skipper's boots. Good luck to him, we had all felt like doing that at some point during that memorable season.

Two more goals – from Finnieston again, and Britton – were met with two more pitch invasions. Eventually, the frustrated referee threatened to call the game off if there were any more repeats, and McCreadie had to retrieve the microphone he'd been using pre-game to make an impassioned plea to the supporters to stay off the pitch. At that point in his life, Eddie could have told the supporters to jump off the East Stand roof and we'd have done it, so staying off the pitch as Finnieston wrapped up the scoring with his hat-trick goal was an absolute cinch.

Of course, an almighty pitch invasion followed the final whistle but we had to get to Putney, for a family gathering at my other nan's home. We were very late getting there, but I suspect not as late as we might have been if a couple of thousand people hadn't been having a massive party on the Chelsea pitch as we headed back to the car.

No sooner had Eddie McCreadie led Chelsea back to the promised land of Division One, than he left the club following a disagreement with the board. It was one of the finest examples of Chelsea Football Club shooting itself in the foot, and there have been many to choose from. The charismatic Scot left these shores disconsolately, pitching up in the United States of America. It would be forty years before he returned to the UK (but more of that later).

McCreadie's successor was his former Stamford Bridge full-back partner, Ken Shellito. Sadly, Chelsea's return to the top-flight lasted just two seasons and ended in an ignominious relegation at the end of 1978/79, but Shellito did oversee one memorable FA Cup victory at the start of 1978 and perhaps the greatest comeback win of all towards the end of that year. What follows are two pieces I wrote for the CFCNet website, run by Norfolk's finest Blue, Peter Sampson, in 2008, relating to Shellito's finest managerial triumphs. I am including them here and they appear consecutively purely by coincidence, as they cover the next two games I will remember all my life.

MONDAY 27TH FEBRUARY 1978

FA Cup Fifth Round (Replay)
Chelsea 1 Orient 2

We buried my nan this week. She passed away a couple of weeks ago, and on Tuesday we gave her a much-deserved final send-off. Naturally it was a sad occasion for those of us present, but in reality this was no time for self-pity, rather an opportunity to celebrate a life very much fulfilled – after all, my nan was well into her 95th year when she took her final breath.

Born and raised in Newcastle, she remained a proud Geordie to the end, even though she died in the Putney flat she had called home for the last forty years. As the hearse slowly made its way round the courtyard outside her flat, as she embarked on her final journey, I stood solemnly with myriad thoughts and recollections vying for a place inside my head; of the patch of grass just yards away which was once a football pitch to my brother, cousins and I, but would now only be able to accommodate a couple of us at a time, as our waists have expanded as quickly as our ages; of numerous drunken renditions of The Blaydon Races, as yet another family function reached a boozy conclusion; of my favourite Geordie pensioner pogo-ing along with me and my brother in her flat on New Year's Eve 1977; and of Orient in 1978. That's right – Orient in 1978. The relevance? Well, you see, before last Tuesday, Orient in 1978 was the last time I could remember standing outside my nan's flat with a lump the size of a golf ball in my throat.

It had all been going so well. Mind you, it didn't seem as much when the draw for the third round of the FA Cup had pitted Chelsea against current English and European champions Liverpool. The Blues, struggling to make any kind of impact in their first season back in the top-flight after a two-year sojourn into the Second Division, had battled manfully to keep their heads above the relegation zone, while the Reds – en route to a second successive European Cup triumph – continued to flourish. Worse still, on the morning of the big match, news filtered through that due to injury, the home side would have to do battle with their mighty opponents without the services of three of their most influential players: defensive titan Micky Droy, the versatile Kenny Swain, and Ray Wilkins, captain and stand out star of Ken Shellito's young side. Veterans Charlie Cooke and Ron Harris stepped into the breach, while

Clive Walker, an exciting but inexperienced young winger, with just nine previous appearances to his name, was included in the starting line-up. In contrast, Liverpool manager Bob Paisley was able to name a team comprising ten full internationals, with fearsome midfielder Jimmy Case the odd one out.

Having missed out on a magnificent treble the season before, after losing to Manchester United in the FA Cup Final, the Reds were determined to go one better in 1978. Forty thousand Chelsea fans took their places on the terraces and in the stands, more in hope than genuine expectation, but early tensions were eased considerably when Walker sprinted past his marker, future Chelsea hero Joey Jones, and unleashed a scintillating shot that swerved away from Ray Clemence's outstretched hand before nestling in the top corner of the England custodian's net. One-nil to the mighty Blues, a lead that was comfortably protected until half-time – and was then quickly trebled after the break.

It was super sub Steve 'Jock' Finnieston – deputising for the knackered Charlie Cooke – whose low shot doubled Chelsea's lead, followed just a couple of minutes later by the goal that sent forty thousand fans delirious, Tommy Langley latching on to Phil Neal's under-hit back pass and sweeping the ball past Clemence. As the ball hit the net, Langley sprinted excitedly towards where my dad and I were standing near the bottom of the Shed End terrace, before being mobbed by team-mates. They were just a matter of yards from us and we could have almost reached out and joined in the celebrations. Mark Worrall, David Johnstone and I were talking to Tommy last weekend, and had it not been for the presence of my fellow Blues, I may have struggled to resist the urge to grab our former striker and continue a goal celebration that began more than thirty years ago.

A Kenny Dalglish header gave the visitors brief hope, but when burly target man Bill Garner set up Walker for an easy finish, the game was over. David Johnson scored a late second for Liverpool, and their odious captain, Emlyn Hughes, embarrassed himself with a laughable attempt to earn Garner a red card, but nothing was going to spoil this day. On the contrary, the fact that Hughes' childish histrionics were ignored not only by the referee but also by a set of team-mates who had little time for him, only served to delight the home supporters more.

The fourth round draw served up a home tie with Division Two side Burnley. However, freezing temperatures caused the postponement of the clash at just ninety minutes' notice. My dad and I just went back home, but a few hundred Blues' supporters decided to head north... to

Highbury, where Arsenal's clash with Wolverhampton Wanderers was guaranteed to go ahead, thanks to the Gunners' much-vaunted, smarty pants undersoil heating. Commentating on the game for *Match of the Day*, John Motson became hilariously confused when, midway through the first half, a sea of blue and white scarves appeared in the North Bank, accompanied by a throaty roar of 'Chelsea'.

Three days later, Burnley were dispatched in style. Despite the concession of a first minute goal, Shellito's boys continued what had been a free-scoring month for them with an almighty 6-2 triumph, which came hot on the heels of five-goal performances against Birmingham City and Ipswich Town. And they were sharing the goals around, too, as six different players – Droy, Wicks, Wilkins, Langley, Swain and Walker – got on the scoresheet against Burnley. Suddenly people were starting to sit up and take notice of Chelsea's young team... so what happened next was inevitable, really.

The Blues already knew when they beat Burnley that their fifth round opponents would be Orient. This would be a revenge mission for a Cup embarrassment at Brisbane Road six years earlier, when Dave Sexton's King's Road mavericks were sent packing at the same stage by the lowly East Londoners. Returning to the rundown Leyton ground, Ian Britton, a squad player at the time of the 1972 defeat, almost struck a spectacular goal, when his 30-yard thunderbolt was superbly saved by the Os' goalkeeper John Jackson. As thousands of visiting fans rose to celebrate what looked a certain goal, a small wall collapsed. Fortunately, nobody was injured, which was a miracle in itself considering the amount of young fans who were standing at the front of the terrace when the wall gave way.

The replay was played on a Monday night. My aunt and uncle were over from Australia and were staying with my nan at her flat in Putney. We had been round to visit at the weekend and my uncle had expressed an interest in coming to the replay with my dad and I. We met him at the ground, confident that his first ever football match would be a joyous occasion for the three of us. However, on reaching the Bovril Gate, we found people were queueing into the Fulham Road. Twenty minutes later, we had just managed to get past the Fulham Road pavement and onto the cobbles of the much-loved entrance to our beloved Shed terrace. We heard the teams being announced, and we stood patiently in line. We heard the cheers of the fans as the players ran out onto the pitch, and still we stood patiently in line. We heard kick-off, throw-ins, free-kicks and corner kicks being awarded, and still we stood patiently in line. And then, with more than thirty minutes played, some big skinheads started to kick up a fuss. Suddenly, the big steel gates that loomed over the Bovril entrance creaked open, and in we all ran.

Within seconds of reaching the Shed and finding a suitable space at the back of the terrace from where we could watch the game, Chelsea were gifted the lead by Orient defender Bill Roffey, who inexplicably but expertly lobbed the ball over his own keeper from a tight angle.

We'd only been on the terraces for a couple of minutes when the half-time whistle blew, but we'd seen what we'd come to see: Chelsea had scored and now had one foot firmly in the last eight of the FA Cup.

Of course, it all went pear-shaped in the second half. Orient's Peter Kitchen, a striker who sported a Zapata moustache that made him look like Tucker from *Citizen Smith* (that's one for the oldies!), suddenly burst into life after the break. I could barely see what was going on out there on the hallowed turf of Stamford Bridge, but my dad swore blind that Kitchen was offside when he scored the equaliser (I have since seen the goals from that night on a compilation DVD and can confirm that my dad was absolutely right, although to be fair to the linesman, Kitchen was only offside by about five yards! Not that I'm bitter or anything).

The inevitable second followed, this time a legitimate strike from Wolfie Smith's friend and fellow member of the Tooting Popular Front, and Chelsea were out. My dreams of Wembley were shattered – it hadn't occurred to me that the likes of Arsenal, Ipswich and West Bromwich Albion were still in the competition, waiting to shatter my dreams anyway. In my juvenile mind, victory over Orient would have guaranteed us the trophy.

We jumped in the car and made the short journey to Putney to drop my uncle off at my nan's flat. My dad told me to stay in the car as he popped in to see my nan and to say his goodbyes to my aunt and uncle, who were leaving for home later that week. While he was gone, I thought about the match I had just witnessed, the sheer injustice of the defeat (because as a kid I NEVER accepted that Chelsea deserved to lose any game), and the abuse that I knew would be coming my way less than twelve hours later in a Shepherds Bush school playground that was riddled with QPR fans. My eyes filled with water, a lump burned in the back of my throat... this was pain on a grand scale.

I'll never go to that flat in Putney again, so perhaps I can now bury the pain of Orient in 1978, and start to get on with the rest of my life.

SATURDAY 14TH OCTOBER 1978

Football League Division One
Chelsea 4 Bolton Wanderers 3

For a while during the 1970s, Frank Worthington was the coolest man on the planet. At least, that's what I thought. He was a striker with sublime skills and outrageous levels of self-confidence. His beautifully coiffured hair and fulsome moustache combination was straight out of a barber's window, and his stylish fashion sense certainly did a great job of concealing the fact that he was actually from Halifax. Oh, and the birds – as they were called back then – loved him. He might have only ever played for crap clubs, as I saw it back then (Huddersfield, Leicester, Bolton and Brighton to name but a few) but wherever he plied his trade, the supporters took him to their hearts. And why did he only ever play for crap clubs? Because the man whose autobiography was titled *One Hump or Two?* failed a medical through high blood pressure when Bill Shankly tried to take him from Leicester to Liverpool. The reason for his high blood pressure on the day of his medical can be derived from the title of his book.

Worthington was already approaching veteran status when he appeared for Bolton Wanderers in the season of 1978/79, but the immaculate skills remained. Early in that campaign he scored the goal against Ipswich Town for which he will always be remembered: as a ball was partially cleared from a set-piece to the edge of the Ipswich box, Worthington collected it with his back to goal and indulged in a quick spot of keepy-uppy, before flicking the ball over his own head and swivelling to rifle a sweet left-foot volley into the bottom corner of the net. Sublime.

In December 1978, my school in sunny Shepherds Bush was given a batch of tickets for a match between QPR and Bolton at Loftus Road, and I was one of the lucky ones to be invited along. It was a grey, cold day and Wanderers led 2-1 as an uninspiring game reached its closing stages, when Worthington, who already had his name on the scoresheet, decided to liven things up. Receiving the ball forty yards from goal, the big striker turned past one mesmerised defender and twisted past another before unleashing an unstoppable shot past Phil Parkes in the Rangers goal. He celebrated with a slide along the turf on his knees directly in front of where I was sitting in the South Africa Road Stand. At that moment, I wanted to *be* Frank Worthington.

Later that evening I was wandering along Kensington High Street on my way to a disco (oh, how very 70s) in a church hall, and as I sauntered past the Royal Garden Hotel, who did I see in the forecourt but Mr Frank Worthington, all suited and booted and no doubt waiting for some glamorous female companion to arrive. I never got within fifty yards of him, but some of his magic must have rubbed off because there were two 'birds' at the church disco that I fancied, and that night I snogged them both. It might have all been very innocent in hindsight, but at the time I felt like a 13-year-old Oliver Tobias! Cheers, Frank.

Prior to Bolton's trip to Loftus Road, their last visit to west London had been a couple of months earlier, and although Worthington almost certainly didn't let the result spoil his Saturday night on the town, that match in October would prove to be one of the most incredible ever seen at Stamford Bridge.

There's no disguising it: Chelsea were crap in 1978/79. Bolton arrived at the Bridge having already knocked the Blues out of the League Cup courtesy of two Frank Worthington goals to one Tommy Langley strike, and at half-time in the Stamford Bridge clash, the Trotters led by three goals to nil. Of course, Frank had scored one of them – a penalty – and the other two had been notched by Alan Gowling, prompting the question to the former Manchester United man: Why the long face?

With twenty minutes remaining, and the score unchanged, manager Ken Shellito made the most inspired substitution of his disappointing tenure. He sent on his twelfth man, Clive Walker – sporting an outrageous tight perm that he can only dream of these days – and watched his super-sub turn the game in a flash. You see, when you're writing about Walker, you simply have to slip in a reference to flashing somewhere in the piece. It would be rude not to.

Five minutes after Walker's introduction, Tommy Langley scored what appeared to be no more than a consolation, before Kenny Swain swept the ball home from ten yards to put Chelsea within a goal of the visitors with eight minutes remaining. Three minutes from time, Walker sprinted past Bolton's right-back, Paul Jones, and slotted the ball beyond Jim McDonagh to bring the scores level, and send the vast majority within the twenty thousand crowd delirious. But there was more to come. In the final minute, Walker found himself one-on-one with Jones again. The Chelsea man knocked the ball past his opponent and sprinted beyond him, before sending in a low cross which was shanked into his own net by that star of *Panorama*, Sam Allardyce.

The final whistle blew seconds later, and hundreds of fans raced onto the hallowed Stamford Bridge turf to celebrate the Blues' third win of the campaign with their heroes. The fourth win came at Manchester City in December, but victory number five did not follow until April, by which time Chelsea had been relegated back to Division Two, eventually ending the season with a miserly 20 points. You see, Chelsea really were crap in 1978/79. And so was I on the day of that famous 4-3 win over Bolton. And this is why...

Sadly, despite already being a regular at the Bridge by this time, I had to miss the Bolton match for a pretty bizarre reason: my nan was getting married! And as if missing out on the comeback of the century wasn't bad enough, I didn't manage to cop off with even one girl, let alone two, at the reception that night. Now, it's pure speculation of course, but I just wonder what might have happened had I been in the same location as Frank Worthington earlier that day. You know what? I bet I would have been beating them off with a stick!

SATURDAY 17TH MARCH 1979

Football League Division One

Chelsea 1 Queens Park Rangers 3

My dad had been a match-going Chelsea supporter from his young, post-war days growing up in West Kensington. He had seen the Blues' first League Title triumph in 1955, and told me about the likes of Stan Willemse, who he said was hard as nails. Throughout the 1960s and through to the middle of the 1970s, my dad also frequently went to away games, including midweek, and I would often wake up the following morning to a note telling me how Chelsea had got on the previous night. He was a Chelsea Pools agent in the early 1970s and it is fair to say that the passion I have had for Chelsea throughout my life is something I caught directly from him.

Sadly, through his job as a milkman my dad developed significant back problems at a relatively young age. Not only did it cost him his health, it also cost him his job. And it cost Chelsea one of their most loyal supporters. As the 1970s drew to a close, my dad was standing in pain at Chelsea games on a crumbling, half-empty terrace, watching sub-standard football. Finances dictated that upgrading to a seat in one of the stands was not an option, so it was the terraces or nothing. As a passionate follower of the likes of Roy Bentley, Peter Osgood and Charlie Cooke, watching the Blues meekly surrendering week after week must have been heartbreaking. As far as I am aware it was not a conscious decision, but when a QPR side which would join Chelsea in the relegation places at the end of the season won handsomely at the Bridge in March 1979, it proved to be the last game he would go to for 35 years.

Reflecting the importance of the fixture, there was a crowd of 25,871 inside Stamford Bridge, 25,871 of whom were supporting the home side as the visitors' fans continued their cherished tradition of being elsewhere whenever their team was playing Chelsea. For me, the day had started early as I had heard the news that Peter Bonetti and Peter Osgood, the latter midway through a brief and ultimately unsuccessful attempt to rekindle former glories in SW6, would be attending the opening of a petrol station opposite the West Brompton cemetery gates in Fulham Road.

Arranging to meet my dad at 2pm outside the Bovril Gate, I headed off alone to watch what I assumed would be a grand opening with large crowds, witty speeches, some music and perhaps a few freebies. When I arrived, however, I realised I was confusing it with the Radio One Roadshow. Schoolboy error, albeit that I had the excuse of still being a schoolboy.

With a scrap of paper and a pen in my hand, I fought my way past nobody to where the two Chelsea stalwarts were speaking to a petrol dignitary. He was quizzing Bonetti about his recent announcement that he would be retiring from English football at the end of the season, to head for a new life north of the border. I remember vividly that the fuel fool asked if Bonetti would really be quitting this time, as he had threatened to do so previously only to change his mind. Even as a 13-year-old I thought this was a cringeworthy query, given that our superstar goalkeeper would be 38 later that year. Still, I listened intently as Bonetti politely stated that he would definitely be leaving, and I then pounced when an opportunity arose. Thirty seconds later the deal had been done. The two Peters had signed my piece of paper, seen my face light up and turned back to their conversations with the grown up. They were both perfectly polite, but they would never have known that they could have actually had a more mature conversation about their careers with me.

With the grand opening not quite fulfilling my expectations – although destiny would dictate that I would finally get to a Radio One Roadshow in Great Yarmouth that summer, and meet Simon Bates (I didn't bother with the pen and paper) – I found myself with the best part of three hours to spare. I could go back home or hang around Stamford Bridge, penniless but not penless, until my dad arrived at 2pm. I think I must have figured that I was on a roll when it came to buddying up with my Chelsea heroes that day, so I stayed put. My dad arrived at 2pm, by which time I had given up on any hope of a wave from Gary Stanley or a "My word, young man" from Ray Wilkins.

Despite being cheered on by only the contents of their dugout, QPR were much too strong for a truly dreadful Chelsea that day. My dad, brought up on a diet of quality players from the likes of Roy Bentley and Jimmy Greaves through to Ron Harris and my two new mates from the petrol station, was now standing in pain, both physical and emotional, as he watched his beloved Blues hurtling towards relegation with a centre-half pairing of John Sitton and Mike Nutton, a bloke called Jim Docherty chasing his own shadow around the pitch, and the aforementioned Chopper Harris playing as the falsest of false nines. The visitors won 3-1. Chelsea were relegated back to Division Two a few weeks later, finishing bottom of Division One with a total of just twenty points from 42 games. Dad was out of here. Division Two, here I come.

SATURDAY 25TH OCTOBER 1980

Football League Division Two
Chelsea 6 Newcastle United 0

Chelsea did their best to climb back into the top-flight at the first time of asking, but it wasn't to be. A calamitous Easter – not the last time they would suffer that fate in the 1980s – saw points dropped which would ultimately cost them a return to Division One by the slimmest of margins: goal difference. By the time the 1980/81 campaign began, the Blues, now managed by Geoff Hurst, were again seen as front-runners for promotion, so a 2-2 home draw with Wrexham on the opening day of the season was a major disappointment. However, things were about to get far worse, and when West Ham beat Chelsea at the Bridge courtesy of a last-minute Graham Wilkins own goal on 6th September, Hurst's men sat third from bottom in Division Two, with a total of just three points from their first five games.

Thankfully, autumn 1980 brought a huge turnaround in fortunes for Chelsea. Beginning with a single-goal victory at Cambridge just a week after the Hammers had held sway in SW6, the Blues embarked on a run of nine wins and two draws in their next eleven games. The scorer of the goal which sparked the run, Colin Lee, would find the net eleven times during that run of games, and four more in the five that followed. However, his finest individual performance that season came when Newcastle United visited at the end of October.

Having won at Orient courtesy of an outrageous, 35-yard thunderbolt from Mike Fillery in midweek, Chelsea were now in fifth place. The Geordies, who had been swept aside 4-0 in the same fixture the previous season, were always one of the more attractive opponents during the Blues' dark years of Division Two, but unlike the previous season when they arrived at the Bridge in top spot, this time around they were rooted in mid-table. Chelsea, however, were now flying and, fittingly, were largely doing so from the wings as Lee's prolific spell in front of goal was assisted in no small manner by magnificent service from out-and-out wingers Phil Driver and Peter Rhoades-Brown.

Newcastle were no match for the Blues that day. In front of the BBC *Match of the Day* cameras, Chelsea tore their visitors apart with a virtuoso performance that, in my mind at least, was one of the best of the decade. Lee profited three times from magnificent wing-play to score a stunning hat-trick, with Fillery, Clive Walker and a sensational team goal finished by Gary Chivers, which would eventually be placed second in *Match of the Day's* Goal of the Season competition, completing the scoring. So comfortable was the win that when John Bumstead felt a little discomfort late in the game, Hurst decided to complete the match with just ten players, having used his substitute a little earlier.

The following day I checked into Charing Cross Hospital for some minor surgery on an ingrown toenail. In another example of how the world has changed, I would spend five nights in hospital, four of which were for recovery from the routine operation. It was a boring week, but it didn't feel that way when I arrived on my ward and was shown into the TV room. *Match of the Day*, which was being shown on Sunday afternoons at the time, came on the telly box and I was very pleased with myself as I announced that I had been at the game we were about to watch when it took place 24 hours earlier. There was a general consensus that I was lucky to have witnessed that performance first-hand.

I left hospital the following Friday, and that evening Chelsea won 1-0 at Cardiff with a goal from debutant Chris Hutchings. The following weekend, Colin Lee was again the hero as Oldham Athletic were beaten by the same score. My toe was still bandaged, so I couldn't wear shoes and therefore had to miss the Oldham game, but I had a follow-up hospital appointment the following Wednesday evening, the same day on which Chelsea would be hosting Derby County at 7.45pm. Chelsea were on fire and I was desperate to be there, so I took a pair of shoes along with me, said a prayer, rubbed the genie's lamp, threw some salt over my shoulder and when the huge bandage was removed and replaced with a small one that meant I could put my shoe on, I knew I would be at the game that evening.

Dropped off at the ground by my mum directly from my appointment, I hobbled into Stamford Bridge and reluctantly took my place on the terrace at the front of the Shed, where the view was so poor that few people ever stood there unless they had to. If it was raining, nobody stood there unless they had a toe to protect from danger. That night I hobbled home wet and wearily, having stood in pouring rain for ninety minutes as the Rams burst the Chelsea bubble with a 3-1 win. The 6-0 humbling of the Geordies ten days earlier already seemed a lifetime away. I'd grown a new toe and everything since then. Two and a half weeks later, on the last weekend of November, John Bumstead scored Chelsea's last away goal of the 1980/81 Division Two campaign.

From December to May, the Blues scored in just three of their last 22 League games. But blimey, that autumn was good. And that performance against Newcastle was sublime. I'll remember it all my life. And the kindness my mum showed me over that whole period, ferrying me to and from hospital, visiting me daily, bringing me gifts and, of course, giving in to my protestations and taking me to Stamford Bridge for that Derby game when she really didn't think it wise, will never be forgotten either. God bless, Mum. I didn't always deserve your love and compassion, but I always got it.

SATURDAY 13TH FEBRUARY 1982

FA Cup Round Five

Chelsea 2 Liverpool 0

If you can't score goals, you don't win games. And if you don't win games then there is only one trajectory you can follow. The post-autumn goal drought of 1980/81 cost Geoff Hurst his job, and the angry response of the Chelsea supporters led to the departure soon after of chairman Brian Mears. A Blues side which at one point seemed certainties for promotion, ended the season in 12th place in Division Two. The final game of the campaign saw Notts County comfortably brush Chelsea aside at the Bridge, as they celebrated being one of the clubs who took advantage of the home side's inability to maintain a promotion push. The game ended with more fans on the pitch than players, and the departure of the chairman – grandson of the club's first and founding chair, Gus Mears – was probably inevitable.

Mears' last act as chairman was to recruit former Wrexham and Middlesbrough manager John Neal as Hurst's successor. A quietly-spoken Wearsider, Neal had replaced the popular Jack Charlton at Ayresome Park following a successful spell in North Wales during which lowly Wrexham earned a reputation as accomplished giant-killers in domestic Cup competitions. With a promotion also to his name at the Racecourse Ground, Mears hoped that Neal was the man who might fire Chelsea back to the big time. In his first season at Stamford Bridge, the new manager would write another chapter in his own book of impressive Cup upsets.

If the infamous tribulations of Chelsea's previous campaign didn't dissuade Neal from moving south, he would certainly spend the first few weeks of his time in charge learning a lot about where the club now found itself: a mid-table Division Two side who were capable of performances ranging from the sublime to the ridiculous, with the latter becoming a stronger forte than the former. So it was that in the last few days of October 1981, Neal's side deservedly dumped high-flying Division One Southampton – Kevin Keegan and Mick Channon amongst their number – out of the League Cup on a memorable night in SW6. Three days later, a largely unchanged Blues team slumped to the single most ignominious defeat in the club's history, when they were rolled over 6-0 by Rotherham in a Division Two clash. It has emerged in recent years that goalkeeper Petar Borota had 'taken drink' in the Millmoor changing room before kick-off, and again at half-time. It has also emerged that despite an official attendance of 10,145, there were actually more than 50,000 visiting fans present that afternoon.

Chelsea's 1981/82 FA Cup campaign got off to a late start, inclement weather either side of Christmas meaning they didn't even know who their opponents would be until Hull City beat Hartlepool United two days after the scheduled third round day. Two weeks later, on a bitterly cold Monday night, the two sides played out a goalless draw, before the Blues emerged triumphant from a replay three days later. Less than 48 hours after that game, and with 17-year-old goalkeeper Steve Francis still bearing facial cuts after having a bottle thrown at him by Hull supporters as the team coach made its way back to London, Neal's former side Wrexham, featuring future Chelsea heroes Eddie Niedzwiecki in goal and Joey Jones in defence, held the Blues to a goalless draw in the teams' fourth round clash. By the time the tie was resolved in Chelsea's favour following two replays in North Wales, the Blues knew their reward for success would be a visit from European Champions Liverpool. Unlike four years earlier when Ken Shellito's side had beaten the Reds, this time they would be taking on Bob Paisley's men as a struggling, mid-table Division Two team. Surely lightning couldn't strike again?

Inevitably there was a full house inside Stamford Bridge for the fifth round clash. At a time when football hooliganism was rife and Chelsea supporters' reputation was more brutal than most, it was rare that many clubs brought big numbers of followers to SW6 (unless it was for a visit to Craven Cottage, of course, which was very much at the opposite end of the boisterous spectrum). However, Liverpool garnered support from all over the country and there would always be a reasonable number of them present at away games. It was no different on this occasion, although the welcome they received from home fans on the North Stand terrace led to the kick-off being delayed by a few minutes, the teams having to retreat to the changing rooms before the referee had even tossed his coin. Having been stood on the Shed terrace for well over an hour before the game took place, I had watched the ground fill; heard the raucous, intimidating reception given to the visiting Liverpool players as they inspected the pitch in their suits; seen the terrace opposite explode into a mini war zone; and then settled down when I saw the best team in Europe take to the pitch, resplendent in their all-red kit, ready to destroy my ridiculous hopes of a Chelsea win. After all, if Rotherham could put six past our defence, surely Ian Rush could do that on his own.

What transpired on the pitch that day will never be forgotten – it's a day I'll remember all my life. Within ten minutes of the game starting, Peter Rhoades-Brown pinched the ball off professional Scouser Terry McDermott – all permed hair, moustache and cheeky banter – before racing away to fire past that paragon of virtue, Bruce Grobbelaar, to send the Bridge into a raucous frenzy. Rhoades-Brown's breathless celebrations are now iconic, and although by his own admission the young left winger could be a little erratic, that moment defines his Chelsea career for many.

With stellar performances from everybody in a blue shirt, but with particular credit going to young goalkeeper Francis and the two Colins – Lee and Pates – the former who never gave the Liverpool centre-halves a moment's peace, and the latter who clipped Graeme Souness' wings all game, Chelsea sealed a memorable victory when Lee took advantage of another Phil Neal gaffe at the Bridge and rifled home the clincher. The last few minutes were a glorious celebration, the packed Shed full of flailing arms, stranger-hugging and loud vocal tributes for eleven true blue heroes.

Like so many wannabees at that time, I owned a green flight jacket which I thought instantly made me look threatening. My nine-stone frame and desperate attempts at being a pretty-boy undoubtedly held sway though, and nobody on earth felt threatened by me. The day after that game, I decorated the back of my flight jacket with a drawing of a gravestone and the words 'RIP Liverpool'. Worse still, I carried on wearing it for a while, so if you recall a skinny boy who carried zero threat, walking around West London thinking he was prettier than he actually was, that was me. Thanks for tolerating me during that 'unusual' phase. You probably should have beaten me up.

MONDAY 27TH DECEMBER 1982

Football League Division Two
QPR 1 Chelsea 2

The occasional Cup giant-killing aside, there was very little to get excited about as a Chelsea supporter in the early part of the 1980s. There are lots of nice memories, many of them undoubtedly enhanced by time, but the records show that this was a bleak period in the history of Chelsea Football Club. Entrenched in the second tier of English football, still feeling the pinch from the East Stand redevelopment a few years earlier which left the club in huge debt, and with home support dwindling, even if the numbers following the team away from home remained impressive, it was hard to disagree with the tabloid newspapers' much-beloved 'Club in Crisis' label being attached to Chelsea.

For my part, having just celebrated my 17th birthday when the 1982/83 season kicked off, I still threw the weight of all my support behind anybody who wore the blue of Chelsea. But despite the glorious naivety of youth, there were clear signs of cynicism encroaching into my thoughts. I was still young enough to have 'favourite players', one of whom remained Clive Walker, who had held that status with me ever since he burst onto the scene a few years earlier. But John Bumstead had also crept onto the page, and possibly even was starting to surpass Walker in my affections. Walker's ability to get the supporters on their feet as he raced past defenders made him an obvious choice for a young lad to get excited by, but I'd also started to acknowledge that he didn't do those things quite as often as I'd convinced myself, and in fact for every outstanding Walker performance there would be three or four shockers. Johnny Bumstead, on the other hand, didn't have shockers. You got a minimum 7/10 performance from him in every game, and he chipped in with his fair share of goals – some absolute belters amongst them. Bumstead often played alongside his old mate Mike Fillery in midfield, and Fillery was probably the most naturally-gifted player at the club. He had the proverbial 'wand of a left foot' and when he could be bothered, was a joy to watch. But despite all his talent and my fondness for flair players, Fillery never fully won me over. The reason? Because even at that young age, I had picked up the impression that he didn't really care. Didn't really care for becoming better than he already was. Didn't really care for putting in the effort to supplement his natural ability. Didn't really care about Chelsea Football Club. With hindsight, I was starting to view Walker similarly.

In terms of final placing, 1982/83 is the worst season in Chelsea's history. Only four Division Two teams finished below them that season, and but for Walker's stunning strike in the penultimate game at Bolton, the Blues might have been kicking off the following season in Division Three. Worse still, so perilous were the club's finances at the time that they may not have kicked off the following campaign at all. Had John Neal not returned to Wrexham and brought Joey Jones down south at the end of October 1982, I have no doubt in my mind whatsoever that relegation would not have been avoided.

Jones wasn't initially a popular choice when he joined. A few run-ins in previous games, ironically often with Walker, had him marked down as something of a villain in the supporters' eyes, and I was one of many who had reservations about him coming to Chelsea. Some went as far as to send threats to the Welshman, which was certainly a few steps too far, but it was clear that the fans would take some persuading before he won us over. Getting sent off on his debut at Carlisle might have won him a few cult hero points had Chelsea managed to win the game, but it was another one that ended in defeat.

When Bolton Wanderers arrived at the Bridge for the last game before Christmas, the Blues kicked off in 16th position. The team were struggling, the few fans who were still turning up (there were less than seven thousand in for the Bolton game) were becoming increasingly disillusioned, and a cloud had descended over Stamford Bridge and wasn't planning on going anywhere soon. And then Jones took a kick to the head as he threw himself into a ruck of players in front of the Shed End goal. He'd taken that kick because he'd rather get hurt than see Chelsea concede a goal. He cared. Better still, he refused to leave the pitch despite blood seeping from a head wound. The terraces had a new hero.

The next game was at Loftus Road, against a QPR side managed by Terry Venables. The best team in the division by a distance, Rangers had narrowly lost to Spurs in an FA Cup Final replay at the end of the previous season, and were now on their way to winning the Division Two title and promotion back to the top-flight. A year and a day earlier, Chelsea had played on the ridiculous Loftus Road plastic pitch for the first time, and had somehow hit the dominant home side with the ultimate smash-and-grab as two late goals sealed victory. It seemed unlikely that a repeat would happen this time, but the usual Chelsea hordes had taken control of Loftus Road off the pitch, and those boisterous supporters raised their voices further when the teams ran out and Jones applauded them all, then gave a gesture which said he was going to get stuck into the QPR side. From that moment on and for the remainder of his career, the Chelsea supporters were eating out of Joey's hands.

For me personally, QPR away was always my favourite game of the season. My local club, the one most of my friends supported, the one that played in the ground I walked past on my way home from school every day and laughed at their tinpot stadium. I loved going there with Chelsea, standing or sitting where we wanted, taking advantage of the generosity of their supporters who always had to be elsewhere for that particular fixture. But I'd missed the game the season before because my parents took us away for Christmas, and I'd seen Chelsea there four times in the previous decade only to witness three draws and a defeat. I'd never seen us win at Loftus Road before.

When Tony Sealy opened the scoring for Rangers midway through the first half, it was hard not to feel that the match would go to form, and that the home side would be too strong for the visitors. However, within five minutes Walker had levelled for Chelsea. And as Joey had predicted, we were having a real go. And it was another player who enjoyed a battle, David Speedie, who put the Blues ahead early in the second half, when he headed home a pinpoint cross from Peter Rhoades-Brown to send the majority inside the stadium wild. The best team in the division were being outplayed. Chelsea didn't just hold out for the three points, they kept taking the game to the home side and played them off the park. It was no coincidence that when the final whistle blew, the Rangers defenders were retreating as Chelsea ran at them in search of a third goal. They say you never forget your first time, and that win in W12 was very sweet indeed.

It was quite a rare thing but I went to that game with my two oldest and closest friends, Patrick and Simon, neither of whom supported Chelsea. But they celebrated with me when the goals went in, and we all embraced when the final whistle blew. The only thing we took exception to was the entire away end singing along to Phil Collins at half-time. However, as abhorrent as that was, it shouldn't detract from what was a memorable game, and one that the three of us still talk and laugh about to this day. It's just a very happy memory, one of many I have from Shepherds Bush days if I'm honest. A piece of my heart will always belong to the place, just not to its football team.

SATURDAY 27TH AUGUST 1983

Football League Division Two
Chelsea 5 Derby County 0

"Only the very young and the very beautiful can be so aloof, hanging out with the boys all swagger and poise." So sang Tom Robinson on his seminal track *War Baby*. Released in the glorious summer of 1983, it stood tallest of all amongst a mountain of top-quality tunes to reach the airwaves that year. I remember the first time I heard it played, thinking it was incredible and rushing out to buy it. Little did I know that some of his "swagger and poise" was about to rub off on my beloved Chelsea, who just weeks earlier had dangled a foot into the depths of Division Three.

I think it's fair to say that for a number of my early years, I thought I had drawn the short straw somewhat. I had no say in falling in love with Chelsea Football Club, but I had done so at an unfortunate time. The Blues had won the FA Cup in the months before my first game, and the European Cup Winners' Cup a few months after. I had no recollection of the first triumph and only vague ones of the second. The first Chelsea Cup Final I clearly recalled was the shock League Cup defeat by Stoke City in 1972. After that, the club's fortunes went into freefall and I spent the best part of a decade watching defeat after defeat, with the exception of one season, 1976/77.

As the summer of 1983 hit our shores, bringing with it glorious sunshine and searing temperatures, Chelsea Football Club had reached its lowest point. In May, on the penultimate weekend of the 1982/83 season, a single-goal victory at Burnden Park, Bolton was all that stood between the once-mighty Blues and a first ever sojourn into the third tier of English football. We eventually finished fifth from bottom in Division Two, the club's lowest ever placing.

That summer I got myself a full-time job to make a few quid during football's off-season, and to help feed my addiction when it returned at the end of August. It was the first time I had dedicated an entire summer to working, and it was just my luck that I did it in a year when the British weather matched that of the Mediterranean. The job was a strange one, based in a dry cleaning sweatshop for a firm who only took private bookings, primarily from wealthy customers, the most famous of whom were Paul and Linda McCartney. My best mate, Simon Bailey, worked there and got me the job. It was located in a large, uncompromising unit underneath Ladbroke Grove tube station. There were some nice people who worked there, including Simon, but they were comfortably outnumbered by knobheads. One of the latter became my line manager, and because he had a talent for manually removing stains from rich people's clothes, he had quite rightly developed a level of arrogance to suit his immense ability. I could only dream of one day being that talented.

I hit 18 that summer, too. There was a general election a month before my birthday, so I was literally five weeks away from being trusted with the vote. Madness. I have no idea who I would have voted for or why, but I suspect if there was a candidate who supported Chelsea, he or she would have been the one, regardless of their policies. If the Monster Raving Loony Party candidate was Chelsea, I'd have happily had him in Number Ten. As it turned out, the only person who actually got my vote that summer was my new girlfriend, whose brother, Steve Kersey, I had loosely known as a fellow Blue for a few years. Steve and I would become much closer friends over the coming year as he joined Keith and I in travelling home and away, to watch Chelsea play out what would ultimately become my favourite season.

The previous season had been statistically Chelsea's worst ever, and had ended with supporter discontent primarily being aimed at manager John Neal. In the summer of 1983, Neal and his assistant, Ian McNeill, put all of their critics – and I was one – back in our box when they completed the most extraordinary regeneration of their team using just under £500,000 of Ken Bates' hard earned fortune. Out went a few of the players who were either not committed enough, not good enough or a mixture of both, and in came Eddie Niedzwiecki, Nigel Spackman, Kerry Dixon, Pat Nevin and Joe McLaughlin. At the behest of the chairman, two former heroes of the Blues' early-70s glory days also returned, the ever-smiling, ever-optimistic John Hollins as player/coach, and the ever-bitter Alan Hudson, who had more in common with those who had just been released than with those who'd been newly recruited.

The sun was still beating down hard as the season kicked-off. I had left a two-week family holiday early to come home for the start of the season. I felt bad and a little ungrateful doing it, but it ultimately proved to be an inspired decision. The new signings had generated a fair level of excitement in and around Stamford Bridge, but Chelsea were no longer considered likely promotion candidates as had previously been the case when most of their Division Two campaigns commenced. Even within the club there was no pressure on Neal and his men to challenge for promotion this year – there was a two to three year expectation to achieve this laid out by chairman Bates. Confidence was certainly higher at Derby County, though. The Rams had beaten Chelsea three times last season, and arrived at the Bridge on opening day amongst the bookies' favourites to go up. Managed by Brian Clough's former right-hand man, Peter Taylor, and featuring two League and European Cup winners during the pair's time at Nottingham Forest, Archie Gemmill and John Robertson, Derby were highly fancied. Which made Chelsea's extraordinary start to the 1983/84 campaign all the more breathtaking. The Blues blew the Rams away with an exhilarating performance. One new boy, Spackman, opened the scoring in just the fourth minute, and another concluded it with a personal brace – Dixon scoring the first two of what would ultimately be 193 goals in a Chelsea shirt. In between the new signings finding the net, stalwarts Clive Walker and Chris Hutchings also scored. 1983/84 was underway and Chelsea had beaten Derby County 5-0 to set the scene for what would be a great nine months ahead. Hanging out with the boys, all swagger and poise.

SATURDAY 28TH APRIL 1984

Football League Division Two
Chelsea 5 Leeds United 0

By leaving my holiday early at the start of the season, I was not only able to witness the 5-0 destruction of Derby but to also see wins at Gillingham, in the League Cup, and at Brighton. The latter was a bittersweet day that I have written about before, a sensational win over another highly-fancied opponent, a remarkable away turnout from the biggest travelling support in the country, and Paul Canoville flooring an opponent who thought it was a good idea to verbally abuse him. But I also saw a fellow Blue suffer a fatal accident on the way home, when he put his head out of a train window and it collided with a bridge. Almost forty years later, that incident still makes me feel physically sick when I recall it, and I find it difficult to speak about without getting emotional. My thoughts remain with the family and friends of that young man. Likewise, although 1983/84 will always be top of my personal list of favourite seasons, I do also recall another Chelsea supporter, Richard Aldridge, an innocent student from Gloucestershire, who was set upon and killed by cowards at Huddersfield in October 1983 as he made his way back to his friend's car after the Blues' victory at Leeds Road. Again, my thoughts are with the Aldridge family.

Throughout the 1983/84 season, I was part-enduring/part-enjoying my last year at college. Basically, I was enduring the academic side and enjoying the banter and sport. Exactly how it should be for any immature 18-year-old boy. Remarkably, soon after the season started I managed to get myself an evening job in a new branch of Sainsbury's that was opening in Gloucester Road. I like to think it wasn't remarkable that anybody would employ me as a part-time shelf-stacker, but the remarkable bit was that they needed staff three nights per week: Mondays, Wednesdays and Thursdays. No weekend work, and as most of Chelsea's midweek games took place on Tuesdays that season, only minimal impact on my attendance at games. I couldn't believe my luck, even if I did have to miss a couple of League Cup games and Micky Droy's testimonial.

Chelsea's unexpectedly impressive start to the season continued unabated into autumn and beyond. The previous season had been made worse for me by the success of QPR and Fulham in the same Division

Two from which the Blues almost exited through the relegation trapdoor. The two other West London sides both excelled, Rangers being comfortably the best side in the division and the Cottagers only missing out on promotion when they lost their nerve in the final weeks. Nevertheless, Fulham that season were undoubtedly the best team in SW6, so when Chelsea spectacularly put them in their place with a 5-3 win in the pouring rain at Craven Cottage in October, it was another marker put down by the 'new' Chelsea. Kerry Dixon again scored twice, Joey Jones wildly celebrated his second and last League goal for Chelsea, and Colin Lee continued a good start to the season as Dixon's strike partner, with a neat finish in front of the packed away terrace. But the star of the show that day was the diminutive, boyish right-winger Pat Nevin. An unknown south of the border prior to joining in the summer, this was the day the 19-year-old gave the supporters their first glimpse of the magic and chaos he would create in a Chelsea shirt for that and the subsequent four seasons. Pat scored his first goal for the club that day at Fulham, and a month later turned in one of the greatest individual performances I've ever seen, as Chelsea again dispatched a highly-fancied rival, Newcastle United. Chelsea in the early-80s had a run of high-scoring victories over the Magpies, but the fact that this one – a 4-0 triumph – was against a line-up that included Kevin Keegan, Terry McDermott, Peter Beardsley and Chris Waddle, made it probably the most impressive of the lot. Nevin's own personal performance included 'that run', when he took the ball from his own goalkeeper and slalomed his way to the opposite end of the pitch, probably the most famous unrecorded but unforgettable moment of the modern(ish) era at Chelsea. Nobody who saw that game, has forgotten that moment. Pat would go on to win Chelsea's Player of the Year trophy at the end of that season, and the fact that he came out above a host of other impressive performers – not least the goal machine Kerry Dixon – in the voting tells you all you need to know about the levels he reached that term. He was an absolute joy to watch, and we were lucky to have him.

The only time the Blues began to mis-fire or look vulnerable that season was in December, with defeats at home by Manchester City and Grimsby Town both exposing some vulnerabilities. The loss to the Mariners was of particular concern, coming as it did through the concession of three quick goals after Chelsea had cruised into a two-nil lead. When further defeats followed at Middlesbrough and Blackburn, the latter in the FA Cup at the start of 1984, John Neal moved quickly to sign another of his Wrexham old boys, Mickey Thomas, to add some grit and stability to his side for the second half of the campaign. And what a master stroke that turned out to be, as starting with the Welsh left-sider's winning debut at Derby on January 14th the Blues remained unbeaten for the remainder of the campaign.

A week after Thomas took his bow at the Baseball Ground, he scored two on his home debut to help Chelsea depose Sheffield Wednesday at the top of the table with a 3-2 victory over the Owls, and although the destination of the title of Division Two champions would be unknown until the final day, both Chelsea and Wednesday negotiated the promotion run-in comfortably. For the Blues, a 1-1 draw at Newcastle, against a resurgent United side who would ultimately clinch the third promotion place, was a potentially troublesome hurdle overcome. Three weeks later a somewhat less expected test of Chelsea's promotion credentials came at Cardiff, where the home side led by three goals with just six minutes remaining. The visitors' three goal-salvo in those remaining six minutes may only have been worth a point, but I suspect they may have done much to convince any doubters that this Blues side was made of much stronger stuff than some of its recent predecessors. Sadly, though, I would miss the miracle of Ninian Park due to appearing for the last time in the annual Hammersmith and West London College five-a-side tournament. In my last year of playing in a competition where the standard was always pretty good, my team finally put in a decent run all the way to the semi-finals. I felt surprisingly deflated when we lost that game, not helped by the fact we were ahead 1-0 courtesy of a goal scored by yours truly, before I then deflected in an equaliser which preceded a collapse to defeat. To then get home and hear Chelsea were 3-0 down to Cardiff was a bitter pill to swallow, and when the score remained the same with ten minutes left to play I switched off Dickie Davies and World of Sport to skulk off to my bedroom. A little later I put on the radio for the final scores and my day brightened considerably!

Promotion was virtually sealed when Crystal Palace and Shrewsbury were beaten on consecutive Saturdays. The game at Selhurst Park was another during which the Blues set out their credentials against a side sent out to try to bully them. Palace put the boot in from the off that day, no doubt under the instruction of their manager, Alan Mullery. Even Gary Locke, one of the best right-backs I've seen at Chelsea, resorted to the dark arts that afternoon, and it was painful to see. It was painful to feel, too, for Mickey Thomas when Locke caught him from behind.

Chelsea's first chance to confirm promotion came at Portsmouth, on a Tuesday evening which meant... I didn't have to go sick from work. I was never going to miss this game. That said, for a while I thought I might when an inadequate 'man' in a policeman's uniform decided to arrest Steve and I for singing, along with a few hundred others, "Chelsea boys we are here" as we disembarked from our train. It was utterly bizarre that he singled out the two of us when there were literally hundreds singing. I'm sure the fact that we were both about five foot six and nine stone wet through had nothing to do with it. The uniformed bell end – who was definitely bullied as a child, and also by his wife as an adult – worked for the British Transport Police and was based in Stratford. If anybody knows of a 1984 transport copper who fits this description, please show him this piece and tell him I said hello.

The uniformed cretin aside, this was also an ultimately disappointing night on the pitch. On the cusp of promotion when leading 2-0 in the second-half, the Blues let Pompey back into the game and had to settle for a point. To make matters worse, the local police then decided to start a load of aggro at the end of the game. If my memory serves me right (Spoiler alert: it does) they came a distant second in that particular fight. Which made me smile.

The outcome of the Battle of Fratton – apart from it being the earliest known example of a police force taking the knee when they realised they'd bitten off more than they could chew – was that promotion could now be sealed the following weekend. At Stamford Bridge. Against the old enemy... Leeds United.

I have one simple way of describing Saturday 28th April 1984 when I talk about it. It was 'one of the happiest days of my life'. We've had great days since – quite simply, in more recent times Chelsea have won every club trophy worth winning – but this day was beyond special to an 18-year-old kid with a royal blue heart, who had borne so many disappointments supporting the Blues thus far. Oh, and I got on to the hallowed Stamford Bridge pitch for the first time. And the second time. I hadn't managed it in 1977, when the 11-year-old me had to do as he was told and stay put during the 4-0 win over Hull City. Seven years later, the 18-year-old me had a cuddle with Colin Pates after Paul Canoville scored the last goal of the game, and a few moments later I went back on for a party when the final whistle blew. Keith and Steve were on there with me and none of us would have wanted to clinch promotion any other way. Mickey Thomas had set the Blues on their way with an early blast, before Kerry Dixon notched a stunning hat-trick. Canoville's goal made it 5-0, an emphatic way to seal a return to the top-flight after five years away.

The following Friday, Steve and I travelled up to Maine Road for another trip and match which has become iconic – the 2-0 live televised win over Manchester City. What a night that was. What a season that was. What a fantastic time in my life that was. In my Chelsea-supporting life, 1983/84 never has been and never will be bettered.

SATURDAY 25TH AUGUST 1984

Football League Division One

Arsenal 1 Chelsea 1

I guess the summer of 1984 marked the point at which I had to become a man. At least I think that was what was expected of me now that I had completed my three years at college, and had a diploma and a successfully re-sat English O Level to my name. The world was my oyster with those credentials.

Of course, further education isn't for everyone. Some people work hard at school, take A Levels and then study for a degree for a few years. Others, though, take their school form into their college career, like a lazy footballer who was once being eyed up by Chelsea, but can't be arsed to push himself and spends his peak years in the Isthmian League (there will be people reading this now who know me and are expecting a dig at Micky Fillery, but they'll be disappointed because I wouldn't do that). To be fair, my Isthmian League days at Hammersmith and West London College were a great laugh. I got my Business Diploma at the end of year one. It was the sort of course you passed with distinction as long as you spelt your name correctly on the exam sheet. I passed with distinction. The next two years were spent taking the next level course, Business Certificate, and the O Level English Language retake. I had failed it at school, although it was the only one of my many failures that genuinely surprised me. My name was mis-spelt on the certificate but I couldn't be bothered to query it – all my other results were poor, so what was the point in making a fuss about this one? I actually managed to get a grade U (Unclassified) in English Literature, which I thought was particularly harsh considering I hadn't read any of the books.

So I left college with the world's worst diploma and an O Level that I very possibly already had, and then went looking for a job with about three million others. I had my part-time Sainsbury's work and I fully expected to be taking extra shifts there for at least the remainder of the year, but to my amazement I was successful in getting the first job I interviewed for. What was even more amazing was that I had always wanted to be a journalist. Amazing because this was nothing like being a journalist. I would be starting my working life as a civil servant in the Inland Revenue. Let the games begin. Those three years disrupting lessons and blocking classroom doors with giant notice boards hadn't been wasted after all.

As I was still living at home with my parents, in Studland Street, Hammersmith, all I really needed money for was to pay for my Chelsea addiction. Just as well really, because my first annual salary was in the region of £5,000. It's hard to believe nowadays, but in 1984 that kind of wage was enough to ensure a football-mad manchild was able to watch his team play home and away, week in and week out. And five days after I hit the 5K jackpot, I was on my way to Highbury to watch John Neal's newly-promoted Blues take on Arsenal. It was the same fixture which had confirmed Chelsea's relegation five years earlier; half a decade on, we were back.

25th August 1984 is writ large in Chelsea fan folklore. It was an established fact based on police statistics, that during the previous season, Chelsea's away following was third in size only to Manchester United and Liverpool. It's also an established fact that both those clubs have a wide fan base which spans all four corners of England, and further afield. Chelsea have always had a decent and well-established following in the north of England, but nothing on the scale of United and Liverpool. The fact is, the third biggest away following was also the single biggest travelling support, with the vast majority of Chelsea's travelling army starting their journey from in or around London. And that day, it is estimated that somewhere in the region of 20,000 Chelsea fans took over Highbury in a show of strength which never has been and never will be reciprocated. It's an occasion that warrants the phrase: If you were there, you know.

Well, I was there and I wouldn't have missed it for the world. I had five days' worth of my 5K salary metaphorically in my back pocket, and when Kerry Dixon scored his magnificent equalising goal in front of the massed ranks of blue in Highbury's Clock End, I would have gladly given all 20,000 Chelsea fans present an equal share of my first week's wages. They would have got 0.005 pence each.

MILKING THE 1984/85 LEAGUE CUP RUN

The 1983/84 promotion season will always be my favourite. I had my 18th birthday a month before that season kicked off, and like most 18-year-olds I was having the time of my life. Chelsea's incredible upturn in form came at me fast, and while the previous season's results were the biggest blight on my life at that time, the spectacular reversal the following year gave me more joy than anything else. As Chelsea approached their first top-flight kick-off in six years, I had no doubt whatsoever that the next nine months would be a success, but I had no reason to believe they would be so much fun that the 1984/85 campaign would eventually sit alongside its predecessor in my heart. Chelsea didn't win a trophy that season, but supporting the Blues back then was about so much more than trophies. Having said that, we should have won the League Cup that season and the fact that we didn't will always be something that makes me sad. That was a great team with a great manager, and they deserved a big, winning day out at Wembley.

The highly creditable draw at Arsenal was just the first of many classic games throughout that season, and my Inland Revenue salary windfall ensured I could personally attend many of them. In September, Chelsea embarked on a League Cup run which would eventually comprise a total of ten matches, the last of which would end in mayhem as the Blues fell at the final hurdle before Wembley. I was fortunate enough to be at all ten games, each of which had its own high-drama and moments to treasure. Some had a few moments to dread.

The League Cup at this time was sponsored by The Milk Marketing Board, and the FA had sold out on the name formally so that the proper terminology for it was now The Milk Cup. Before long it had embarked on its own inglorious run of naming and re-naming to the extent that I now insist on referring to it simply as the League Cup, rather than try to research or remember the correct term for every given season. If you're in your fifties it's the League Cup, and Chelsea's 1984/85 run began with a visit from Millwall. Which was nice.

The home leg against the Lions was more straightforward on the pitch than off it. Kerry Dixon scored twice and our former defender Micky Nutton once, into his own net, to secure a routine 3-1 win. If my memory serves me well, I think I slipped out of the Shed and onto the Fulham Road just around the time Millwall's mob made an appearance on the pitch just after the final whistle. That was a somewhat easier journey than the one that took us to The Den for the second-leg, where we had to dodge small groups of scruffy home fans on the pitch-black streets of salubrious New Cross. We had to run a gauntlet to get onto the away terrace, and we then spent the next half-hour looking out over the back of the terrace and watching other Chelsea fans doing the same before they reached the sanctuary of the away end. For those old enough to remember the classic gangs of New York movie The Warriors, that was what we likened it to. “Chelsea boys, come out to play.”

A 1-1 draw, Kerry scoring again to equalise Millwall’s early opener, saw the Blues through to round three. The half-time scenes at the opposite end of the ground, where the players’ tunnel was situated and the Chelsea stars were peppered with objects as they approached it, made us a little nervous for the journey home, but thankfully the away support had swelled in number by that time, including a good amount of the sort of blokes you want around you at times like that. We actually had a more comfortable post-match experience than those trying to attack us before the game did. Famously, Chelsea brought the Old Kent Road to life while we were heading back to Hammersmith.

Next came a visit to Fellows Park, Walsall, where we arrived at the terraces just in time to hear a huge roar which told us the Old Kent Road scenes were now being repeated in the Black Country. When the teams ran out for the start of the game, another roar went up and the entire home end scattered like gazelles (the animals, not the work of art Adidas trainers). On the pitch, however, Chelsea found life a little more difficult, twice falling behind to their lowly opponents and eventually being grateful for Colin Lee’s late, brave header that secured a replay the following week, which was won with three goals in the first 15 minutes.

In the next round, much like in Porto in 2021, it took only one game for Chelsea to dispatch Manchester City, Kerry’s superb hat-trick and Pat Nevin’s very funny penalty miss the highlights of a soaking night at the Bridge, but that night ended in tragic scenes when the scoreboard operator went rogue and flashed up the words ‘WEMBLEY HERE WE COME’. Never, ever do that. It’ll always end in tears.

Unlike the Porto 2021 game, the win in November 1984 ushered in a three-match epic tie with Sheffield Wednesday to take place when the League Cup recommenced in the New Year. The two sides remained tightly matched, following their titanic battle for the previous season’s Division Two title (which, as was the case in Porto in 2021, Chelsea won. Although that wasn’t against Sheffield Wednesday, of course. I just wanted to repeat it for a cheap laugh).

The first of the quarter-final trilogy was played at Stamford Bridge on a Monday evening, and not surprisingly ended all-square. Wednesday took the lead through defender Lawrie Madden before David Speedie levelled matters. The Blues had a great opportunity to clinch the tie at the first attempt, but Kerry Dixon saw his penalty saved, something of a curse for Kerry and a number of his team-mates that season.

With less than 48 hours to make plans for the replay, it was an impressive turnout of approximately 6,000 Chelsea fans who greeted their team as they took to the pitch the following Wednesday evening, as we settled in to watch what would prove to be the most exciting, entertaining and incredible match I have ever witnessed live. Sadly, I also witnessed no shortage of police brutality that night, dished out by the South Yorkshire Police, on a night when we stood on the Leppings Lane terrace. Just saying.

As would be the case in all three ties, Wednesday took the lead. On this occasion, however, they would treble it by half-time. There was clear friction between the sides and the only highlight of the first period for us came as Wednesday defended a corner at our end, and as the ball was swung over, Mickey Thomas hit Wednesday's mouthy midfielder Andy Blair with a peach of a left-hook that flattened the motormouth. Hilariously, it seemed the only three people inside Hillsborough who hadn't seen the punch were the referee and his two linesmen. The Wednesday players had seen it and were screaming at the referee for a red card. Us lot on the Leppings Lane terrace had also seen it and celebrated it like a goal, followed by a chorus of "One Mickey Thomas" which the little Welshman implored us to stop as he realised he was going to get away with it. That Mickey would then score the goal of the night, and Chelsea's equaliser, in the second period just made it all the funnier.

Our support throughout half-time was something to behold. We loved that team and we knew that it was packed with character and determination. We'd gone three down with the last kick of the half, but rather than accept defeat we just belted out song after song throughout the break, so loud that it was picked up in the dressing room, leading John Hollins to tell the team "They haven't given up, now go out and do it for them."

Paul Canoville replaced the injured Colin Lee at the break, and had his name on the scoresheet in little more than ten seconds. Twenty minutes later, Kerry scored and it really was game on. When Mickey pulled us level and ran the length of the pitch to celebrate with us, six thousand heads had completely gone. What a moment that was. It was hard to imagine it could get any better, but it did. With just five minutes remaining, Pat Nevin set Dixon free on the right, and he squared the ball into the path of Canners, who poked it under Wednesday's keeper, Martin Hodge, to spark wild celebrations both on and off the pitch.

The final twist came in the last minute, when Doug Rougvie clumsily tripped Wednesday's Mel Sterland, giving Sterland the opportunity to level the scores from the spot. The extra-time period remained goalless, and yet again the two sides couldn't be separated on the pitch. Off it, some separation was required in the players' bar after the game when Andy Blair and a few of his friends thought about seeking retribution for the Mickey Thomas left-hook Blair had worn earlier that evening. But Mickey had some friends of his own with him, including Joey Jones, and the Wednesday man left the scene quickly. By the time of the second replay, he was waving to Mickey and giving his apologies.

A week later, the epic trilogy was settled by, ironically, a last-minute Mickey Thomas goal. Life was never sweeter. Wednesday had, yet again, taken a first-half lead but some magic from Pat set up David Speedie for an equaliser soon after. For what it's worth, Speedo's goal ranks as my personal favourite of all time. For me, it was more than just a goal, it was a moment in time. A moment that personified the mixture of skill, grace and determination that group of players put into the shirt. It was also a moment that captured me at my very happiest as a Chelsea supporter. That team, that kit, those supporters, that atmosphere. A goal scored by a player I admired, created by a man and magician I adored. Pat Nevin remains one of the best Chelsea players I've ever seen.

Drawn to play relegation-bound Sunderland in the two-legged semi-final, Chelsea were hot favourites to reach Wembley. The other last-four clash was an East Anglian derby that pitted another team that would be relegated at the end of the season, Norwich City, with a very average Ipswich Town side. Confidence was sky high amongst the Chelsea support, but over the two games with Sunderland, everything that possibly could go wrong, did.

As all the stories in this chapter are covered in more detail in my previous book, *Celery! - Representing Chelsea in the 1980s*, I won't go over too much old ground again. However, the first leg on Wearside started badly and went downhill from there. Speedie was suspended and, in the first few minutes, Joe McLaughlin dislocated his elbow when he fell awkwardly on the hard and icy surface. The pitch was unplayable, although the same for both sides, and the game would never have gone ahead nowadays. Dale Jasper, impeccable in his first-team appearances to date, replaced McLaughlin from the bench and conceded two penalties, both contentious. Eddie Niedzwiecki saved one, but was beaten when a mis-hit rebound bounced up and over his head. As if all that wasn't enough, Colin Lee and Mickey Thomas both picked up injuries as the Blues played most of the second period with just nine fit men. Off the pitch, I saw police brutality that night which exceeded anything I'd witnessed before, or have seen since. The Sunderland Police Force happily attacked men, women and children that night, and they also played an active part in arranging and executing an ambush of visiting supporters arriving on the official club trains. It clearly took a special kind of lowlife coward to work in the Sunderland Police back then.

The second leg at Stamford Bridge followed an opposite path, starting brightly when Speedie's early goal had the ground rocking with excitement and expectation, before our former attacker, Clive Walker, scored twice for the visitors to effectively seal the outcome of the tie. Unlike many former players in recent years, Walker saw fit to rub his former admirers' noses in it after he scored. At the start of the season when Chelsea opened their home league campaign with a visit from Sunderland, those same supporters roundly applauded Walker when his name was announced in the Mackems' line-up. In his erratic Chelsea career, Walker had included probably the most important goal any Blues player has ever scored, when his thunderbolt at Bolton in May 1983 was enough to save the club from a relegation which might have proven fatal for the entire club. He deserved the applause for that. However, that goal was a moment of magic amongst a sea of dross served up by Walker in that most awful of seasons. In my view, he was clearly one of a small group of players most responsible for the club's plight. Broadly, throughout his Chelsea career, for every moment of Clive Walker magic there was two of utter rubbish. For every Clive Walker goal, there were three missed chances or four crosses into the arms of the ball boys behind the goal. That night, when Walker saw fit to goad the Chelsea supporters who had tolerated his inconsistency for so many years, he discovered just what a stupid thing that was to do when one of them, a chap called John Leftley, stepped out of the West Stand and proceeded to chase him around the pitch. It was a chaotic end to one of the most exhilarating cup runs I have had the pleasure to witness. A sub-plot within a fantastic season when Chelsea and Johnny Neal's Blue and

White Army made their mark on the top-flight all over again, finishing sixth.

By the way, having taken Sunderland to Wembley and a Final clash with Norwich City, Walker, as ever, followed up his glory moment with one of dross, missing a penalty as his side slipped to a 0-1 defeat. How sad.

SUNDAY 23RD MARCH 1986

Full Members Cup Final
Chelsea 5 Manchester City 4

"Tell me mum, me mum,
We won't be home for tea,
We're going to Wem-ber-Lee,
Tell me mum, me mum."

We don't sing songs like that anymore, nor do many of us get the same excitement out of a trip to Wembley as we did back in the days when the Twin Towers remained so elusive. Success has made us this way, so it's not all bad.

1985/86 would be the season when Chelsea Football Club and its supporters finally returned to the stadium now referred to as The Venue of Legends. Proving that title to be correct, Chelsea pitched up with Darren Wood and Doug Rougvie in the team. But more about that later.

At full-strength, the Chelsea side of 1985/86 was a match for anybody, and better than most. But for serious injuries to key players, primarily Kerry Dixon and Eddie Niedzwiecki, that team would have gone very close to winning the League. A late-season implosion and second consecutive sixth-place finish was a poor reward for a side that looked favourites to hit the summit of Division One going into an ultimately disastrous Easter weekend. Liverpool would eventually pip rivals Everton to both the League and FA Cup, the Reds having been lucky to survive a fourth round Cup clash at Stamford Bridge which saw Chelsea play much of the game with just ten men, following injuries to both Dixon and Colin Lee.

The return to Wembley came in a little-known, little-regarded competition called the Full Members Cup. After the tragic events of the Heysel Stadium disaster in May 1985, leading to all English clubs being banned from taking part in European competitions, two new domestic trophies were created. The clubs who had qualified for Europe and were subsequently banned, took part in the Screen Sport Super Cup. Their own clubs having no European football to contest or attempt to qualify for, Chelsea chairman Ken Bates and his Manchester City counterpart Peter Swales cobbled together a motley crew of clubs from the top two divisions to contest the Full Members Cup.

Chelsea's pursuit of their chairman's brainchild began against Portsmouth in front of just seven thousand spectators, an attendance figure similar to most in that competition prior to the Final. Perhaps if it wasn't for another decent run in the League Cup, the Blues supporters may have been more enthusiastic about the Full Members. Having reached the semi-finals the year before, in 1985/86 Chelsea made it to the quarter-finals before losing to QPR. A run which began with a two-leg victory over Mansfield Town, gathered pace after Fulham were dispatched at the second attempt, primarily as a result of Eddie Niedzwiecki producing the greatest individual goalkeeping performance I have ever witnessed. But for Eddie, the Cottagers might have hit double figures that night. Ironically, I almost missed that game. Recovering from flu and off work as a result, I had decided earlier in the day that it would be both unwise and unethical for me to stand out on Craven Cottage's notoriously-freezing riverside away terrace that night. Fortunately I had a last-minute change of heart, quite rightly prioritising Chelsea Football Club over my health and a rare bout of ethical conscience. It proved to be the right decision.

Having beaten reigning champions Everton in the League earlier in the season, the Toffees again came unstuck against the Blues in a fourth round clash which, yet again, went to a replay. Held 2-2 at home in what was a fantastic game of football, Chelsea this time did it the hardest way of all: in a replay at Goodison Park, with ten men (Darren Wood having been sent-off), and with a winning goal scored by the most unlikely of scorers, Joe McLaughlin, in the latter stages of the game.

With that win over an outstanding Everton side, confidence that Chelsea would go at least one step further in this year's competition had never been higher. So some genius quickly re-wrote the lyrics to the 'Tell me mum' song:

"Tell me mum, me mum,
To put the champagne on ice,
We're going to Wembley twice,
Tell me mum, me mum."

Chelsea then lost, after yet another replay, to QPR in the quarter-finals. I blame the idiot who re-wrote the lyrics!

So, inevitably in hindsight, the Blues were reliant on the Full Members Cup for their big day out. For OUR big day out.

An initial three-team group was comfortably negotiated, Pompey being swept aside 3-0 before Charlton Athletic, then playing their home games at Selhurst Park, were beaten 3-1 on a night when the floodlights failed for a while and we all got home much later than planned, cursing the "bloody Full Members Cup." West Bromwich Albion were then beaten on penalties at the Hawthorns, on a night when there were more Chelsea fans cheering on Kerry Dixon in the England number nine shirt in a World Cup qualifier at Wembley, than there were up in the Black Country.

The victory over West Brom saw Chelsea reach a two-legged, regional final. We were CUP FINALISTS. Our opponents would be a very useful Oxford United side, a team enjoying a first season in the top-flight, and which had beaten the Blues at the tiny Manor Ground stadium earlier in the season.

Those two words – Cup Finalists – galvanised a few previously disinterested supporters, and there was a healthy away support at the Manor Ground for the first leg. Surprisingly, Chelsea strolled to an easy 4-1 win that night, despite playing more than an hour with just ten men, after Keith Jones was sent-off for an uncharacteristic lunge at former team-mate Peter Rhoades-Brown. The second-leg saw Oxford pinch a consolation win, but it was Chelsea who advanced to a National Final meeting with Manchester City at…

"Tell me mum, me mum,
We might be home for tea,
Bates hasn't booked Wem-ber-lee,
Tell me mum, me mum."

So after all that, we were told that Bates and Swales were 'negotiating' with the FA on a venue for the Final. *They* wanted it to be at Wembley. *We* wanted it to be at Wembley. There were just no guarantees the FA wanted it played there. There was also the small matter of a Football League season taking place, with very limited opportunities to play the game on a Saturday.

Eventually, after a surprisingly anxious wait for all concerned, confirmation was received that the FA had agreed that Wembley would host the 1986 Full Members Cup Final on Sunday 23rd March. Both finalists would be expected to fulfil their League fixtures 24 hours prior: for Chelsea a visit to Southampton; for City the small matter of a Manchester derby at Old Trafford.

In the build-up to the big day – or big weekend for the many Chelsea boys who either spent Saturday in Southampton, or cheering on the Gers north of the border in the Glasgow derby – the sheer desperation of the Chelsea fans to see their side win a trophy became very apparent. The Blues supporters had snapped up their entire allocation of tickets. 68,000 had been sold in total, and Chelsea had almost 50,000 of them. It was understandable though, the wait for a Wembley visit hadn't been anywhere near as long for City as it had for Chelsea. In the 14 years since Chelsea last played under the twin towers, City had done so four times, twice in the League Cup in the mid-70s, and in the two games which it took to decide the 1981 FA Cup Final.

Once inside the ground, I remember a big crowd of latecomers being shooed into our end from behind the goal. They were lads who had been on the train down from Glasgow, and included my mate Nick Brown. It gave us a laugh seeing them all turn up pitch side. They had witnessed a 4-4 draw 24 hours earlier, so what were the chances of a near-repeat taking place today? And I remember how packed and how loud our end was. It was fantastic. It might as well have been the World Cup Final, you couldn't have squeezed a single person more in there.

The game itself is all a bit of a blur. I recall Eddie Niedzwiecki having to miss out as he was on crutches following the awful knee injury which would ultimately curtail his career. The injury had occurred just days earlier in a midweek clash with QPR, and was a bitter blow to a man who would be voted Player of the Year by the Chelsea fans at the end of the season. Similarly, Kerry Dixon, a player who had been central to all the Blues' success over the past three seasons, failed a fitness test before the game and also had to sit it out. However, Dixon's misfortune gave Colin Lee an opportunity to get some reward for his fierce loyalty and versatility since joining in 1980, and he grabbed that opportunity with both hands.

City opened the scoring early on through Steve Kinsey, but by half-time Chelsea led through goals by David Speedie and Lee. Both our wide men, Pat Nevin and Kevin McCallister (Not that one. That one was taller) were running amok on the flanks, and Speedie's second-half brace completed the first Wembley cup final hat-trick since a bloke called Hurst did it twenty years earlier. Lee then made the score 5-1 to the Blues, and we all wondered just how many we were going to win by. Rather arrogantly, we'd all forgotten Doug Rougvie was playing. City pulled a goal back through Mark Lillis in the 84th minute, which we shrugged off as a mere consolation. Four minutes later, however, a cross was swung to the far post and there was Rougvie jumping higher than all others to plant a header into the net. Past his own goalkeeper, Steve Francis. Not so cocky now. On the terraces we started referring back to a humorous, well thought-out ditty that was regularly rolled out whenever Chelsea were desperately clinging on for the final whistle: "BLOW YOUR F***ING WHISTLE." And then City were awarded a penalty, which Lillis comfortably converted. 5-4 with a minute plus injury-time still to play.

"BLOW YOUR F***ING WHISTLE."
"BLOW YOUR F***ING WHISTLE."
"BLOW YOUR F***ING YYYYYEEEEESSSSS."

Of course, it was never really in doubt, although having just recalled it, I think it best I don't take a blood pressure reading any time soon.

And that was my first time at Wembley with Chelsea. There were better visits to come, but I didn't know that at the time. So when Pates went up to lift the Members Cup, I imagined it was the FA Cup. And I suspect I wasn't alone in that.

In truth, those last few minutes of the game at Wembley were a fair reflection of where Chelsea suddenly found themselves. We didn't know it then, but the following long Easter weekend saw the Blues beaten 4-0 at home by West Ham and 6-0 at QPR. Niedzwiecki's absence was being felt terribly, his replacement Francis, once quite rightly considered England's brightest young prospect in his position, had lost all confidence. When the final whistle blew at Loftus Road, he had conceded 13 goals in 183 minutes of football. John Hollins immediately brought in experienced West Bromwich Albion custodian Tony Godden on loan. Steve Francis never played for Chelsea again, but did inevitably come back to haunt us with a pair of top class performances the following season in the colours of lowly Reading, as they knocked Chelsea out of the League Cup over two legs.

A few weeks after the Wembley triumph, Keith, our mate Colin Savage and I went up to Old Trafford for what looked a crucial fixture for both clubs, both of whom still harboured hopes of a Title win. It was my first time at Old Trafford and I was surprised to see their captain, Bryan Robson, being allowed to referee the game. The programme said the referee was George Courtney, but he was definitely playing second fiddle to Robson.

In recent years, through my friendship with Mickey Thomas, I have met Bryan Robson a couple of times and he is clearly a great guy. I also know what a great friend Bryan was to Mickey while Mickey was fighting cancer, and that kind of support and camaraderie can never be underestimated. He was also a fantastic captain and leader of my country's national team. But when he played for and skippered Manchester United, he wielded a ridiculous amount of influence over referees, and it seemed to me none was more obliging than George Courtney. I can't speak for any other clubs, but I do know that Courtney refereed three games between United and Chelsea, and awarded the Reds four penalties, three of which were highly contentious. He awarded Chelsea the occasional corner and throw-in.

On this night, with United trailing to a Dixon goal at the start of the second-half, Courtney awarded United a generous spot-kick for a Rougvie challenge on Mark Hughes in front of the Stretford End. Jesper Olsen slotted it home, and United were level in a game that both sides needed to win. Thankfully, hilariously and despite the best efforts of a man described by Ken Bates in his next programme notes as a 'homer', Dixon would bring the second period to a close in identical fashion to how he began it, slotting past home keeper Christ Turner to send our immense travelling army back home in jubilant spirits. Even a brick through our train window couldn't spoil our fun – we were just relieved Mr Courtney didn't award United a penalty for it.

Sadly, 1985/86 petered out desperately, climaxing in a 5-1 home reverse against Watford, albeit with Chelsea fielding an injury-hit and unfamiliar team which included 17-year-old one-game-wonder Les Fridge between the sticks. I thought at the time that was the closest I would ever get to seeing Chelsea win the League. To this day, I still believe we could have won it that year but for the injuries we suffered in the second half of the season. Of course, in recent times I have seen the Blues win the Premier League plenty of times, but don't give me any of that 'Where were you when you were shit?' cobblers, because we were invariably in your ground, wondering where you were. And let me assure you that for every one of me, who stuck out the bad old days through to the successful times of 1997 onwards, there are fifty more passionate, more loyal supporters than me, who have put their money where their mouths are, have rarely missed a game in forty years, and have been on every pre-season tour whether it took place in Aberystwyth, Sweden, or on the other side of the world entirely, as the modern Chelsea Football Club seek to grow their worldwide fan base (or, more accurately, the income they can generate from growing it).

SATURDAY 7TH MARCH 1987

Football League Division One
Chelsea 1 Arsenal 0

At this point in my life everything was hunky dory except for my relationship with my fiancée, which was rockier than Rocky 1, 2, 3, 4 and 5 put together. So for some inexplicable reason I, to paraphrase Frank and Nancy, went and spoiled it all by saying something stupid like 'I do'. With those two words I instantly took the leap from immature single young man to immature married young man.

We got married on 31st May 1986. I was 20 and she was 18. We initially rented a flat in Boston Manor, and then bought a tiny one-bedroom shared ownership place in Shepherds Bush, which we moved into on Christmas Eve that year. Seven days later my wife announced that she wanted to separate, and on New Year's Day I packed some things and walked round to my parents' house in Hammersmith. My name and bank details were, of course, on the flat I had been allowed to occupy for a week. But whereas I can look back now and see how cynically I was played, my main concern on the day I left 'home' to return to my real home was making sure I dropped my stuff off in plenty of time to ensure I didn't miss Chelsea's game with QPR that afternoon. And what I remember most vividly about that day has nothing to do with closing a door behind me or shedding any tears, it's the fact that John McNaught scored twice past David Seaman at the Bridge and we beat our local wannabe rivals 3-1. It felt like a good day all told, which tells you much about my level of maturity at that time.

In truth, the glory days of being an avid supporter of Chelsea in that post-summer 1983 period onward were coming to a close. John Hollins had replaced John Neal at the helm, and had brought in an awful coach by the name of Ernie Walley. Despite his goals against QPR, the fact that McNaught was in the Blues' first team was clear evidence of a drop in standards from the three previous seasons. In fact, it was only on Boxing Day – also known as day three of seven in my new home - that Chelsea had beaten Southampton to climb out of Division One's relegation zone.

The upturn in Chelsea's fortunes over that Christmas and New Year period drew to a halt at Luton, where my personal turbulence continued unabated. I went to Bedfordshire's beauty spot with my mate Colin

Savage, and I think it's fair to say both of us were struggling a little at that time with internal strife, anger issues and a propensity to sail a little close to the wind. We had met through work, as we both had jobs in the same building on Shepherds Bush Road, and then bumped into each other in the Shed at Stamford Bridge one Saturday afternoon. Colin lived with his elderly dad in a flat in Acton. I lived wherever I was welcome. Colin's dad was a lovely bloke but had fathered his only child relatively late in life, and then Colin lost his mother. Colin was a few months younger than me, so barely out of his teens and going through a difficult period. Neither of us were 'football hooligans', but we'd both grown up at a time when football matches were regularly the venue of serious punch-ups. As Chelsea supporters, I think we also often felt that we were invincible. At Luton that day, we got well and truly caught out.

Luton's odious club chairman and future Tory MP, David Evans, had introduced a ban on visiting supporters to Kenilworth Road. It was a sensitive arena ever since Millwall fans had run amok there in 1985, but Evans' continual pompous grandstanding on top of his clear intention to give his club an unfair advantage on the pitch, made them a loathsome club at that time. In addition to a stadium composed of only home supporters, The Hatters also played on a ridiculous plastic pitch that many clubs found tricky to master. Unsurprisingly, Luton enjoyed a particularly successful period by their standards during this time. Nevertheless, Colin and I were determined to be inside Kenilworth Road on 3rd January 1987, and we had little doubt that hordes of other Blues would be there too. After all, as everybody knows: You can't ban a Chelsea fan.

By the time Colin and I left to go back to London that day, we had walked from the station to the ground, three times around the town centre, and in and out of various establishments looking for friendly faces with spare tickets. We'd also been inside a police van, inside Luton Police Station and, had it occurred nowadays, would have spent a night in hospital being checked for concussion. The problem was, at the first sign of a big mob (25-30 of them) Colin was attracted like a magnet. The other problem was that Colin hadn't been going to Chelsea anywhere near as long as I had, and I didn't recognise a single one of these guys. Despite me desperately trying to get Colin to walk away, he was smitten and, needless to say, within seconds of welcoming Colin into their firm these brave lads were piling into the two of us. I took a proper kicking from them, curled up in a ball while they took turns at putting the boot in. As they walked away, they told us they were the Luton MIGS.

Annoyingly, they never had a spare ticket for us.

My year had got off to the worst kind of start. On top of my personal difficulties, I had already broken my New Year's resolution, which was to avoid getting a kicking from a small, inconsequential firm, based in a town twinned with my local refuse dump. I had actually quite fancied my chances of seeing that one through, but three days into 1987 and I was already hoping my resolutions for 1988 would be more successful.

As luck would have it, news of our mauling had reached QPR's mob, largely because Colin and I were both friends with one of their main faces, and when Luton were drawn to play their arch rivals of the time, our local club QPR, in the FA Cup a few weeks later, we were told scores had been settled on our behalf. Not condoning it, just mentioning it. And smiling while I do so.

Colin and I didn't miss many games – as long as tickets were available – around this time, and in our current 'angry young man' dual mode, we became increasingly irritated by the unnecessary demise of our team on the pitch. In fact, we became downright militant. Taking our lead from an old friend of ours, Adam Porter, we decided that John Hollins and Ernie Walley had to go, and we were the boys to galvanise the supporters against them.

Adam also worked in the same building as Colin and I but, unlike us, he was in a dead end job only until he achieved his goal of becoming a journalist. In 1983, following a riot down in Brighton when Chelsea played at the Goldstone Ground at the start of September, Adam had contacted one of the tabloids to give them the inside track on the Chelsea Anti-Personnel Firm. The tabloid hungrily absorbed the information, and wrote a salacious piece asking 'Who are the Chelsea APF?' Any similarity between Adam's own initials and those of 'Anti' and 'Personnel' were purely coincidental, of course. Adam went on to be a lead writer in Loaded magazine, famously writing and publishing a piece on John Spencer where they visited the Gorbals area of Glasgow together. Spenny's stock was high at the time, in the wake of his wonder-goal in Vienna, and Adam's timing and inside track on Chelsea was perfect. The inside track came because Adam also used to pen the Stamford the Lion column for kids in the old Bridge News. That particular role came to a juddering halt after Stamford produced a slightly rambling, somewhat off the wall piece one month which slipped the editorial stage and went out in all its drug-hazed glory. The following month, Stamford's child-friendly ramblings were brought to us all by a different writer.

Colin and I had always loved Adam's APF creation and the way he had used it to wind up a tabloid. We used his model to create the Chelsea SBF, apparently a group of supporters who had formed a pressure group with the intention of removing Hollins and Walley from their posts, before they destroyed all their predecessors' hard work which had made the Blues a top six English club again. Ahead of the home match with Arsenal on 7th March, we printed a few hundred leaflets for distribution in various pubs before kick-off. The leaflets said 'THE CHELSEA SBF SAY HOLLINS OUT - PROTEST ON SHED END CONCOURSE AFTER THE GAME'. In midweek, Arsenal had beaten their biggest rivals, Spurs, to reach the League Cup Final, which they would go on to win. Chelsea, on the other hand, went into the game in poor form and with an injury crisis which meant Hollins had to field an unfamiliar team, which included a recall up front for Colin Lee alongside young Colin West, making his first-team debut. There seemed little hope of a Chelsea victory. Naturally, Chelsea being Chelsea, they pulled an unlikely win out of the bag. West, who would go on to have a shortlived but, I thought, pretty decent spell in the first team, scored a belting goal after two minutes which sealed all three points. Proving that above all else, Colin and I were really just two blokes who loved Chelsea, we celebrated West's goal and the final whistle like we had won the FA Cup, even though we knew those two events marked the demise of the Savage and Barker Firm. We did have a sneaky look around the Shed End concourse after the game, but it was just a sea of happy faces, including ours.

A few weeks after that Arsenal game, QPR met Luton in a League match at Loftus Road. There was a huge confrontation that evening in St Pancras Station, and Colin managed to get himself arrested and assaulted by a police dog in a van on its way to the station. In court the following Monday morning he was fined £100 for his part in the shenanigans, to which he had pleaded guilty even though he was adamant that the diatribe he was accused of calling out to a Luton fan just before his arrest – I saw it and it read like Shakespearean prose, it would have taken him half an hour to deliver it – was quite obviously a load of old Jackson Pollocks, concocted by one of Her Majesty's good old boys in blue.

Fine paid and guilt admitted, that should have been the end of the matter. However, a few weeks later Colin and his elderly dad were awoken in the early hours by a police raid on their flat. The coppers rifled through the premises and were particularly interested in a couple of hundred 'Hollins Out' leaflets which referred to a new firm in town: the two-man Chelsea SBF, who's only key encounters to date had seen them take a battering in Luton and a bloody nose from their own team winning a London derby against Arsenal. Fortunately, try as they might, the Met Police were unable to pin anything further on us, largely because there was "nothing to see here" as far as we were concerned. They had a go, though, re-arresting Colin and trying to force him to give them names of other people who were at St Pancras after the QPR v Luton game. In the good old tradition of 1980s policing, their actions were proven to be illegal and the second case against Colin, which was openly and blatantly an illegal one, fell apart on those very grounds. The SBF had disbanded just after full-time in the game against Arsenal, and reverted back to just plain old Colin and Kelvin. John Hollins and Ernie Walley remained in their posts for another year, before Walley was shown the door, followed soon after by Hollins. Chelsea were relegated at the end of the 1987/88 season, just as the SBF had predicted.

SATURDAY 15TH APRIL 1989

Football League Division Two
Leicester City 2 Chelsea 0

When I left my flat in Shepherds Bush on the morning of 15th April 1989, destination Leicester where I had never seen Chelsea win, I was anticipating a day of unbridled joy and celebration. I could never have imagined what would ultimately transpire that day, initially at Filbert Street as Chelsea were denied any prospect of a win by a very dubious performance from the officials; and then at Hillsborough, Sheffield, as news filtered through which rendered any skullduggery at Leicester entirely irrelevant.

The Full Members Cup triumph in 1986 was really the last hurrah for the team first rebuilt by John Neal, then swiftly dismantled by his predecessor, John Hollins. The late-season collapse following that game was a sign of things to come, and two years later Chelsea were back in the Second Division. It looked a highly improbable task to achieve relegation with such a strong squad of players, but Hollins and his deeply unpopular assistant, Ernie Walley, managed it.

After a slow start to the following season, not helped by a six-game closure of the Stamford Bridge terraces following trouble at the play-off final, second leg against Middlesbrough in May, the Blues, now managed by Bobby Campbell, suddenly found their rhythm and eventually cantered their way back to the top-flight, eventually finishing 17 points clear of their closest rivals, Manchester City, at the top of the table. I enjoyed that season but I didn't love it the way I had the 1983/84 campaign. This promotion was more functional, more ruthless, but far less surprising. It was achieved by a group of players who should never have been plying their trade in Division Two in the first place.

There were some good away trips that season, a 2-1 win in the pouring rain against a strong Watford side was particularly impressive, and there were a pair of big wins at Stoke and Oldham that caught the eye. On a personal note, my away match attendance was now becoming affected by the mortgage millstone tied round my neck, and a salary that didn't allow for too much frivolity in my life. Getting to home games wasn't a problem, but as the season reached its latter weeks, I had to decide between a midweek trip to Brighton or the following Saturday's game at Manchester City. I could only afford one, and based on my visits to both grounds in our last promotion season, both had huge appeal. I eventually plumped for a trip to the seaside, where Kevin Wilson scored the only goal of a game from which Brighton deserved more, and may have won but for the impressive form of new signing Dave Beasant between the sticks for the Blues. It was a good trip with Keith, we went early and spent some time in town and on the pier, then joined up with about five thousand fellow Blues in the evening. Three days later, in what has again become an iconic awayday for Chelsea on Moss Side, eight thousand Chelsea – but not me – saw Bobby's boys race into a 3-0 lead before City scored two late goals ("BLOW YOUR F***ING WHISTLE") to give the final scoreline a somewhat skewed appearance.

Stretching my pennies like Bob Cratchitt at Christmas, I managed to get to the next three aways. Ipswich was a very similar affair to Brighton, the home side largely on top but Beasant repelling all they could throw at him. There was a massive turnout from Chelsea that night, and hilariously some home supporters pretended they wanted to pile into us when we celebrated wildly Gordon Durie's late and lucky winner. The Tractor Boys – with the emphasis on 'boys' – were dismissed with little more than a few shrugs and some general laughter.

The games were coming thick and fast, and Chelsea kept winning them. By the start of April, it had become simply a case of 'when' Chelsea would be promoted. There was no longer an 'if'. In a crazy game at The Hawthorns on 8th April, the Blues beat West Bromwich Albion in front of another enormous away following. It was a crazy game, the Baggies taking an early lead before Graham Roberts and David Lee turned the game on its head. The home side then had the temerity to equalise, so Kevin McCallister went straight up the other end and made it 3-2 to Chelsea. And all of this before half-time.

The second period remained goalless, and the result left Chelsea needing just one more win to be assured of promotion. The only blight on that really enjoyable day was a dangerous crush on the packed away terrace, where far more visiting fans had been accommodated than the home club had obviously anticipated.

And so to Leicester. Unsurprisingly, something in the region of eight thousand Chelsea supporters descended on the East Midlands, for a fixture that was always a popular one. There was the inevitable tension in the air (there's a reason why this was always a popular fixture with the Chelsea fans, who only ever got to meet their Foxes counterparts once a season) but I just wanted to get into the ground and onto the terrace, to bag myself a good spot from where I could celebrate promotion. I'd stood on that terrace enough times to know how dangerous it could be when it was busy, and this day it would be busier than ever. As it happened, the scenes from seven days earlier at The Hawthorns were repeated. The away terrace was packed to the rafters, it was dangerous, it was oversubscribed. It was an accident waiting to happen. It could have been us that day. There by the grace of God.

Once the game kicked off, on a warm day and in a red-hot atmosphere, it quickly became apparent to many of us that something wasn't quite right. The home side were getting some strange decisions given in their favour, linesman's flags were going up when they shouldn't have, and being kept below the waist when they should have been waving. Chelsea players were picking up soft bookings, whereas Leicester's over-aggressive right-back, a two-bob Rottweiler by the name of Ally Mauchlen, was running around like a headless chicken, kicking anything that moved but seemingly immune to any sanction.

The fourteen-man Foxes failed to take advantage of their numerical advantage in the first-half, which remained goalless. During the break, an announcement was made that the FA Cup semi-final between Liverpool and Nottingham Forest at Hillsborough had been delayed due to crowd behaviour. Cue much laughter – it was assumed by all that Forest and Liverpool were having a punch-up.

The second-half of the game I was at was an absolute disgrace. Having taken the lead soon after the restart, Leicester were awarded a penalty they didn't even appeal for, when Graham Roberts won the ball from an opponent with a tackle reminiscent of Bobby Moore's on Brazilian Jairzinho in the 1970 World Cup. The referee pointed to the spot and Joe McLaughlin told him he would cause a riot if he carried on. Joe was booked. Gary McCallister's penalty was saved by Beasant. Moments later, Gordon Durie raced forward on the left, and pulled the ball back into the box for Kevin McCallister to run onto and fire home. Cue bedlam in the away end. And then it happened… the linesman raised his flag and indicated that McCallister was offside. Cue bedlam again in the away end, but of a different kind.

Five minutes from time, Leicester sealed the game when their striker Nicky Cross, standing all alone in the Chelsea half except for goalkeeper Beasant, received a forward pass from McCallister and raced through to score. But he was the only outfield player in Chelsea's half, so it was unquestionably offside. Oh no, this time the linesman involved kept his flag down. Peter Nicholas called the referee something appropriate and was immediately sent-off.

For many years after, I wondered what had really happened that day. Until relatively recently, I always considered it the only time I genuinely believed the result of a Chelsea game had been fixed by the officials. Eventually light was shed on the events of that day by Dave Beasant, who in his autobiography described how the referee, a Mr Tom Fitzharris of Bolton, had instructed the Chelsea players before the game that should they win and clinch promotion, they must immediately leave the pitch and not acknowledge the travelling fans. The players, quite rightly, refused. Fitzharris, aided by a local police officer, then said as a compromise that the players could wave to the supporters from the halfway line. Again, quite rightly, the players refused. With that, the result of the game was apparently (and allegedly) decided.

As we left the ground, initial anger at what we had seen was quickly replaced by shock at the news emerging from Sheffield. I clearly recall that at the point I walked out of Filbert Street, reports said three Liverpool supporters were dead. That fact alone shocked me, and many others clearly felt the same. Three deaths on a football terrace was massive news. It was a tragedy, no doubt about it.

I walked back to the station in a convoy while fights were breaking out all over the place, and sirens wailing. I just wanted to get on the train out of there. I'd gone up on the Chelsea Special, and although I'd travelled alone (Colin was banned from games for a period following his arrest) I knew I'd either bump into someone I knew or get chatting on the journey back. As it was, though, there wasn't a great deal of chatter on that homeward journey. People were huddled around radios, gasping at updates coming in from Hillsborough, learning more about the scenes we'd been oblivious to as we stood and swayed on that dangerously oversubscribed Filbert Street away terrace. There was an impromptu collection arranged by the stewards on that train, and everybody gave what they could in the hope that it might in some way help the families of the bereaved. It's hard to imagine, but definitely not hard to believe, that those families and the people who were responsible for the torture and torment they have endured for the past 33 years and counting, will never receive the justice they deserve. It stinks.

SATURDAY 7TH APRIL 1990

Football League Division One
Chelsea 1 Luton Town 0

One of the things I'd always wanted from life was to have a son or daughter who followed in my footsteps in supporting Chelsea. They didn't have to be as excitable as me about it – frankly I would prefer it if seeing the Blues beaten at the weekend didn't ruin their entire week – but the day a child of mine walked into Stamford Bridge with me for the first time, I knew it would make me proud as punch. Before that could happen, of course, I needed a child.

Despite our ups and downs, my first wife and I remained together as a married couple for just under five years. In my eyes, and speaking only for myself, two good things came out of that marriage: 1) I got my mistakes out of the way in marriage number one, so that the real love of my life didn't have to tolerate them in marriage number two; and 2) We had a beautiful son who I have loved and adored since the day he was born.

My wife got pregnant in the summer of 1989, and the baby was due around 23rd March 1990. When Chelsea played Arsenal at Highbury on 17th March, I found out the number for Arsenal's stadium and told her that if there was any inkling of the baby arriving, call them and get them to make an announcement. I knew it was unlikely to happen, but I nevertheless toyed with the idea of giving the game a miss to be on the safe side. As it happens, there was no movement on the baby front and I was present to see Chelsea win at Highbury for the one and only time, despite attending that particular fixture on numerous occasions. It was rarely a happy hunting ground for us, so being there the day Johnny Bumstead scored the only goal of the game was lovely.

Daniel John Barker eventually arrived on the evening of Friday 6th April 1990. They kicked me out of Queen Charlotte's Hospital in Hammersmith just after midnight, and I was back for the start of visiting hours the next morning. I was booted out again at midday, so back-from-his-ban Colin and I headed over to Fulham Broadway to wet the baby's head before Chelsea played Luton Town that afternoon. Chelsea won 1-0 courtesy of a goal from Gordon Durie – yeah, I know – and I then dashed back home to ensure I made it to the hospital in time for the next visiting hours start time of 6pm.

The football, in truth, was very much an aside that day. It was irrelevant in the grand scheme of things, but there was a game that took place, even if I remember nothing about it. All that mattered was that my first child had been born, he was healthy, and was going to be Chelsea. That last one, I'm afraid, was never in doubt.

WEDNESDAY 18TH MARCH 1992

FA Cup Round 6 Replay
Sunderland 2 Chelsea 1

March 1992 and I'm a weekend dad. My marriage is over and I'm back living with my parents in Hammersmith. It's not the first time this has happened but in our hearts, we all know it's the last. A line has been crossed that there's no coming back from.

Work keeps me busy during the week. I'm working at a film company, United International Pictures, also based in Hammersmith. It's full of good people, and fortunately I have a lot of support from some truly great friends there. Most weekends Daniel comes to stay and I slip out on Saturday afternoons to see Chelsea play, while my parents look after my little man. Chelsea Football Club has never been more important to me than it is now – it's my only release from the tension of getting divorced and coming to terms with the fact that at 26 years of age, I'm already about to become a divorced father of one. And I'm acutely aware that all who are close to me can see how hard I'm finding life right now.

Chelsea had reached the semi-finals of the League Cup a year earlier, but had succumbed to eventual winners Sheffield Wednesday. It was another huge blow, and another case of the Blues crumbling to defeat by a team in a lower division. Now, in March 1992, Chelsea had reached the last eight of the big one, the FA Cup, and been drawn at home to Division Two side Sunderland. Having already comfortably navigated a potential banana skin tie at Hull, and then seen off Everton and Sheffield United, hopes were high that our time had come at last. That elusive FA Cup Final was within reach.

The Chelsea side of this time was packed full of experience, including three of Wimbledon's FA Cup winning side of 1988: Vinnie Jones, Dennis Wise and Dave Beasant. With the likes of Paul Elliott, Kerry Dixon, Clive Allen and Andy Townsend alongside them, this looked for all the world like a team that knew how to win the big pots. And even when Sunderland snatched a late draw in the game at the Bridge, few people gave them much chance of winning the replay at their own Roker Park ground.

By the time the game on Wearside took place, the sides knew a semi-final against Norwich City would be the reward for victory. The other semi-final was between Portsmouth and an unusually average Liverpool side. The FA Cup was very winnable this year.

I went up to Sunderland with a mate, Steve McNally, who was amongst the funniest people I've ever met. Any time in his company always flew by, and I would spend most of it crying with laughter at his antics. It was a good journey up there on the train, and definitely a significant release from the rigours of my current situation. As the game kicked off, I was very confident that Chelsea were about to disperse the looming clouds and I would be on my way to Wembley very soon.

Sunderland scored first through John Byrne, also their scorer in the original game and a perennial plunderer of goals against Chelsea in his time with QPR. However, for the remainder of the match it was one-way traffic, with the Blues creating chance after chance, as Sunderland goalkeeper Tony Norman had the game of his life. And then it happened... with just four minutes remaining, Wisey finally beat Norman and we would be going to extra-time against a team who were there for the taking. It was going to be an even later night than expected, but nobody cared.

Of course, Chelsea never really do things by the script, but what happened that night still hurts now. It shouldn't, not now that I've seen us win everything, but it does.

Sunderland got a corner in the very last minute, and right in front of where we were all massed on the away terrace. As the ball was swung over, Townsend deserted the near post just as Mackems midfielder Gordon Armstrong rose high to head the ball past Beasant, into the very part of the net the Chelsea skipper should have been guarding. From where we were standing, we could see the whole thing unfold. It was one of those moments that seemed like it happened in slow-motion. And it was sickening. Not just for the fans either – in my mind I will always remember the image of Paul Elliott on the final whistle, still looking like a giant amongst men but with a look of devastation on his face that mirrored how I felt at that very moment.

The journey home was better than it should have been. Steve was as sad as I was, but that wasn't going to stop him cheering me up all the way back to London. And he did, he made me laugh all through the night until we eventually reached the Capital at some unearthly hour of the morning. We said goodbye and I jumped on a night bus back to W6. I crept into the house so that I didn't wake anybody, went into my bedroom... and cried my heart out.

SATURDAY 26TH DECEMBER 1992

Premier League
Chelsea 1 Southampton 1

The defeat at Sunderland really hurt. It effectively ended Chelsea's season in March, which certainly wasn't an unusual state of affairs at that time, but my own personal turmoil ensured this one felt worse than all the others. I had been clinging to the hope that Chelsea might be my saving grace, but it wasn't to be. In truth, as much as I was feeling sorry for myself, I had other friends – big, hard blokes – who told me the Roker Park loss upset them in the same way it had affected me. As a group of supporters, we had faith in that group of players to go one step further than most of their predecessors, but yet again we had fallen foul of a giant-killing when a trip to Wembley beckoned. As the saying goes 'It's the hope that kills you'. It was certainly the case in 1992, when we definitely had hope that we finally had a team to take us to the Twin Towers again.

Chelsea's season ended with its then-characteristic whimper, and I have to confess I wasn't really looking forward to the summer months with no Stamford Bridge or away ground to go to and release my tension. There was the European Championships to look forward to, but an England side managed by Graham Taylor and featuring the likes of Keith Curle and Andy Sinton was only ever going to bring one thing home: misery. I needed a guardian angel to appear, and to my amazement when she did, it was one of my colleagues at work who I had been friendly with for the past three or four years, but never thought would ever be more than just a friend. I certainly wasn't much of a catch at that time, with a hairline that was receding at the same rate that my waistline was expanding. And, of course, I was a soon-to-be divorced father of one. Fortunately, when I asked Lisa Mulvey if she fancied coming out with me some time, I think she was just too shocked to say no. She was (and still is) lovely and I was (and still am) punching. But hey-ho, thirty years on and we're still going strong. And whatever happens in this book from this point onwards, Lisa is a part of it. She shared the low points – I recall her in our early days laughing and saying she was "sick of hearing about Sunderland" – and she was very much there when Chelsea's fortunes eventually turned in the right direction.

For our first Christmas together, I took the unusual step of asking Lisa if she wanted to come with me to the Bridge on Boxing Day. It was the inaugural Premier League season and we were playing Southampton. Iain Dowie would be appearing for the Saints, so I hoped she would concentrate hard on him and then see me as some kind of Brad Pitt lookalike by comparison. I didn't consider the possibility that Chelsea's real pretty boy, Graeme Le Saux, might choose that particular day to rip his shirt off and give the girls something to smile about.

As it happens, Dowie was the first player to make his mark on the game when he gave the Saints the lead after just a couple of minutes. The Blues, performing reasonably well in the League up to that point, grew increasingly frustrated as an equaliser eluded them, boiling over with Le Saux's act of petulance which didn't go down well with the male majority inside the ground. I joked with Lisa that it was her fault we were losing, and she reminds me of that to this day. Had she been going to Chelsea as long as I have, she'd have known I was just teasing and that at some point in most games back then, Chelsea would be losing.

On Boxing Day 1992, Eddie Newton came to the rescue with a last minute equaliser. Last minute equalisers are generally celebrated like winners, so Lisa got a few hugs and a few more kisses. She then announced that she could see why I loved going to football, but that she would leave it to me in the future. In Lisa's words, I had been going to Chelsea with my mates for a long time and that's how it should be. It was my time to get out and have a laugh, and to let off steam. And she's never been back. No amount of last minute kisses or glimpses of Graeme Le Saux's chest was going to change her decision.

SATURDAY 19TH AUGUST 1995

Premier League
Chelsea 0 Everton 0

I went to my first football match at the age of five, so in my head that is the age that all kids should be ready. I was, and so should everyone else be. It doesn't matter that 25 years after my first game, the modern five-year-old had a wealth of hand-held toy and game distractions that simply didn't exist when I was that age. No, there's no two ways about it: Five is the right age to start going to football.

For all the years I'd been going to Chelsea, for all the games I'd seen and the numerous seasons when I'd hardly missed a home game, I had never had a season ticket until I got my first one in the East Stand Family Section in the summer of 1995. It was for me and my son, Daniel. He was five.

My first game is iconic to me: I have the highlights recorded from TV, the programme from the game, and the programme from the following home match which includes photos and reports from my first game. Daniel's first game is iconic to him because it featured the debut of his first Chelsea hero, Mark Hughes. And it's iconic to me because it featured the debut of Ruud Gullit. The Ruud Gullit with the dreadlocks, the swagger and the World Footballer of the Year trophy. THE Ruud Gullit, and he was playing for Chelsea.

To be honest, the game against Everton on the opening day of the 1995/96 season was fairly uninspiring. Gullit and Hughes looked a class above their teammates, but a 0-0 draw was a fair result. It was clear that it would take a little more time and a few more tweaks to the line-up before Chelsea became a club worthy of this kind of talent within its ranks. But that came, later that year with the arrival of Dan Petrescu, and the following season with Gullit at the helm, and an influx of foreign stars who would set SW6 alight for the next few years. A golden period was on the horizon, and Daniel was in right at the start of it. He may not have realised it at the time, and he may have spent half of those games with his face in a Nintendo Gameboy, but all these years later he is Chelsea through and through, and he now has his own son, Jacob, who at the time of writing is three years and ten months shy of the optimum age for going to his first football match.

As for my other children, Poppy and Sam. Well, Poppy was a month old when Daniel went to his first game and it was another decade before she joined me for a game at Stamford Bridge, a 3-1 win over Fulham in April 2005 which all but sealed Chelsea's first League Title in fifty years. Not a bad start. However, football was never really a huge passion for Poppy and after a year or so she stopped going to games. And Sam, whose arrival into this world gets a mention in a future chapter, started attending matches in August 2005, two months before his sixth birthday, when a Didier Drogba goal was enough to beat Arsenal. He subsequently sat alongside me at matches for the next 15 years, his junior membership finally expiring during the pandemic at the ripe old age (for a 'junior') of 21.

SATURDAY 17TH MAY 1997

FA Cup Final

Chelsea 2 Middlesbrough 0

The summer of 1994 was a big one at United International Pictures. There were five big weddings featuring six stalwart members of staff, and it seemed that for Lisa and I most weekends that summer were either spent getting married, enjoying our honeymoon, or attending the wedding celebrations of colleagues who were also good friends. The first of the nuptials were those of Paul and Lorna Ramsay, who were and remain amongst our closest friends. Paul is also a huge Chelsea fan, who was a matchday steward at the Bridge when I first met him. When Colin, my friend and colleague Dean Dennis, and I celebrated on the pitch after Wolves were beaten and Chelsea reached their first FA Cup semi-final since 1970 in March 94, I spotted Paul guarding the players tunnel and we had a little celebration of our own. He was clearly in no mood to try and get the supporters off the pitch.

Paul and I both had a feeling that it was no coincidence that Chelsea had finally reached a Cup Final in the same period that our respective weddings would be taking place. We thought it was an omen. More than that, we'd convinced ourselves it was a good omen. Sadly, Chelsea didn't play ball. Well beaten at Wembley by Manchester United, I think perhaps it was just a happy coincidence after all.

In fact, we would have to wait just three more years before the FA Cup dream would finally come true. It had certainly been coming. Finalists in 94, semi-finalists in 96 and a cosmopolitan team which, in truth, cost a lot of money to assemble and was entirely expected to reward the club with some silverware. In 97 it produced.

That wasn't just a very special time in my life, it was one of a few reasonably shortlived golden periods in the history of Chelsea Football Club. The mid-50s and the club's first League Title, the swinging late-60s to early-70s, 1983 to 85, and the sexy football years from 1995 to 2000 would all fit the bill as brief golden eras at the Bridge. 2003 onwards has been much, much more than just a brief and beautiful chapter in Chelsea's history – it has been two decades of almost constant success for a club that has transformed into a behemoth of European football.

Starting with the capture of Mark Hughes and Ruud Gullit, things progressed further when the latter replaced Glenn Hoddle as manager and began to attract some of the cream of European football to SW6. By the time the 1996/97 campaign started, with the newly-appointed Dutchman at the helm, Chelsea could boast a squad which had added the names of Gianluca Vialli, Roberto Di Matteo and Frank Lebeouf to those of Hughes and Gullit. The jewel in the crown, Gianfranco Zola, would join them in November. The team wasn't quite yet at the level to challenge for the Premier League title, but a tilt at a domestic cup competition seemed realistic.

Lisa and I moved to Woodford in early January 1997, just a few days after Chelsea had secured a safe path into round four of the FA Cup with a 3-0 win over West Bromwich Albion. It was a great way to start a new year. We'd previously been living in Stratford, not the nice one known as Shakespeare Country, but the East London version which was more like Shake You Down Country. It wasn't a nice place to live – if the local lowlife wasn't helping itself to the contents of our house, it was stealing the wheels off our car. The move to much leafier Woodford couldn't have worked out better, and those early months in what is still our family home ran parallel to Chelsea's wonderful run to Wembley.

The fourth round draw pitted the Blues against table-topping Liverpool at the Bridge. It would prove to be one of the great Chelsea games of the era. Having already beaten Liverpool in the League earlier in the month, Gullit's men knew they had nothing to fear, but a shambolic first-half showing allowed the visitors to go in at the break two goals to the good. As the players made their way to the tunnel, that nice Robbie Fowler was goading his opponents by showing the score on his fingers. You can buy whole streets in Liverpool, but you can't buy class.

The Chelsea boss made a change at half-time which would ultimately, and quickly, turn the game in Chelsea's favour. Throwing on substitute Mark Hughes, so often Liverpool's nemesis in the past, and switching to a back-three, Gullit totally outwitted Reds counterpart Roy Evans, and within minutes of the restart the Liverpool defence was showing its old vulnerabilities. It was Hughes himself who scored the goal that put Chelsea back in the game, before he set up Gianfranco Zola for a supreme strike to level the scores. Two Gianluca Vialli finishes made the final score 4-2, but when Dan Petrescu used his fingers to point out the score to Fowler and his equally vile strike-partner Stan Collymore, neither seemed to think this kind of behaviour was acceptable now. Funny, that. And yes, it was funny. Very, very funny to see little Robbie's face contorted with anger, squealing (and looking) like a pig because Petrescu had given him a bit back.

Victory over the Reds brought a clash with Leicester City at Filbert Street. Given the Foxes' injury woes on the day the game was played, it should never have needed a replay for Chelsea to prevail. That it did was largely down to the Blues becoming complacent once they led 2-0, and also to a shocking refereeing decision to award a free-kick for a totally innocuous Steve Clarke challenge from which Leicester scored their equalising goal.

The replay at the Bridge has gone down in infamy for the reaction of Leicester manager Martin O'Neill and a press pack who were desperate to see little old Leicester shock Chelsea's band of foreign footballers. The fact that O'Neill sent his team out that night with an instruction to keep eleven men behind the ball and try to nick a penalty shootout was completely ignored. The truth is, they got what they deserved when after almost two hours of ultra-defensive tactics, they were unpicked just three minutes from the end of extra-time by an apparently-controversial penalty decision. Sitting at the opposite end of the ground, in the Matthew Harding Stand, I thought when Erland Johnsen crashed to the ground it had looked an obvious, stonewall penalty. The Leicester players were apoplectic, surrounding the referee and raging at the perceived injustice. I'd like to think Robbie Fowler was doing the same in his living room. Once the furore had died down, Frank Leboeuf nonchalantly struck the penalty past Leicester keeper Kasey Keller, and Chelsea were in the FA Cup quarter-finals where they would play Portsmouth at Fratton Park.

It was only when I got home that night that I learned how controversial Chelsea's late winner had actually been. I left the ground convinced there was no issue with the validity of the penalty award, but Lisa told me it was all over the TV and even on the news that Leicester had been hard done to. I switched on the TV and Spurs fan Danny Kelly was hosting a debate about it where he was Fowler-like in his rage, even going so far as to say that he 'hates' Frank Leboeuf. I seem to recall either Ron Harris or Peter Bonetti, perhaps both, were in the studio with Kelly and defending Chelsea's position. Strangely, there was no such anger about the decision that led to a replay being needed in the first place. The conversation was decidedly one-sided – I wonder why? Up the foreign invasion.

In the days after Erland's hilarious dive, with tabloid rubbish printing stories about Leicester supporters calling in sick from work en-masse due to the stress caused by the referee's performance, I happily got on with the task at hand: getting tickets for the next round. No sick leave needed here.

The Pompey tie was negotiated easily, Chelsea running out 4-1 winners and being drawn against Wimbledon in the semi-finals. The other semi saw Middlesbrough play Chesterfield. Even though the Dons had won at Stamford Bridge earlier in the season, and Boro's cosmopolitan line-up included some outstanding opponents, Chelsea were installed as favourites to lift the trophy.

When Wimbledon had beaten Chelsea on their own pitch in October, they had done so by targeting Chelsea's five-man defence, and in particular the sweeper Leboeuf. The Frenchman was clearly shocked by what the Dons threw at him that day, but the tactic worked. This time, in the Cup semi-final played at Highbury, Gullit would outwit opposition manager Joe Kinnear, removing the wing-backs and switching to a flat back-four. Despite his heroics in the fifth round, Erland Johnsen was not a regular starter for the Blues that season. However, he was restored to the side for the semi, and Chelsea's muscular back-four comfortably dealt with everything the Dons threw at them that day, which wasn't much in truth.

A 3-0 victory in the warm sunshine of Highbury took Chelsea through to a date at Wembley on May 17th. Surprisingly it took a replay before Middlesbrough were confirmed as the other finalists.

Paul and I, and our families, decided to make a long weekend of it when the Cup Final rolled around. We each now had small children, Poppy was born to Lisa and I in June 1995 and Calum to Lorna and Paul just over a year later. As we knew, or at least certainly hoped, we wouldn't be around much on Cup Final day, we all went out together to Thorpe Park the day before. When we had last been at Wembley, for the 1994 Final, it was a miserable, wet day. However, this time when we woke up on Final day, the sun was shining and it was warm. Nothing was going to go wrong today, you could feel it.

A few of us met up for pre-match drinks in Wembley and the atmosphere was electric. After a couple of hours we made our way to the ground, and went our different ways to whichever block we were sitting in. Paul and I were sitting with Dean Dennis, and I think it's fair to say that all three of us were equally excited by the prospect of what lie ahead, having all been there home and away through the dark times in previous years. Even the sight of Cliff Richard flouncing onto the pitch before leading the singing of Abide With Me wasn't allowed to mar the day, and once the teams had entered the fray, met the dignitaries and had a quick warm-up, it was time for kick-off.

A loud One Man Went To Mow was in full throttle in the Chelsea end as the ref blew his whistle, and in traditional style the entire end leapt to its feet as the number ten was reached. A few concluding chants of 'CHELSEA, CHELSEA, CHELSEA' were belted out before a few thousand bums returned to their seats. But like the old hypnotist's trick of convincing a compliant victim that their seat is scalding hot, we all jumped back up in unison as Robbie Di Matteo unleashed a stunning long-range shot over the head of the Boro keeper and into the back of the net. 42 seconds had elapsed and the Cup was on its way back to the Fulham Road at last. It was absolute mayhem in our end.

In truth, the game was a poor one. There was so much continental talent on the pitch, but none really shone to the extent of which they were capable. Boro's Italian super-striker, Fabrizio Ravanelli, left the field early, midway through the first-half, apparently injured and unable to continue. Middlesbrough supporters will be better judges of his character than I am, but it looked to me that he'd let his side down and could have given them a bit more before declaring himself unable to continue. I wonder what his manager, Bryan Robson, made of Ravanelli's apparent eagerness to leave the field in such a huge game.

Another Italian, Gianluca Festa, had the ball in the net for Boro but his header from a set-piece was ruled out for offside. I've seen it a few times since that day and it's a really tight call. However, I truly believe that had Festa's goal stood, Chelsea would simply have gone through the gears and won the game anyway. A week earlier Boro had been controversially relegated from the Premier League, the controversy being as a result of a points deduction from an unfulfilled fixture which the Teesiders strongly contested as simply a miscommunication. As a club, they appeared understandably deflated by recent events, and having lost their talismanic striker so early in the game, it felt that they really were there for the taking.

It took until the 83rd minute for Chelsea to finally put the game to bed, Hammersmith-born (like me, so I'm claiming an assist) Eddie Newton putting the final touch to a flowing move. This goal was scored and celebrated in front of us. It was a magical moment, one that still gives me goosebumps. The same can be said for the post-match celebrations shared between the players and the fans. Nobody in blue was in a hurry to leave the stadium that day, and it's said the celebrations in the ground were the longest ever. There was a lot of pent-up hurt and frustration unleashed that day, and it was dispensed in an outpouring of joy and emotion the likes of which I'd never witnessed before. Even now, if I watch those celebrations I find it very difficult to control my emotions. As days to remember go, there are very few to beat 17th May 1997 for me, and nor will there ever be.

SUNDAY 3RD OCTOBER 1999

Premier League

Chelsea 5 Manchester United 0

On October 3rd 1999, Chelsea played at home against all-conquering, all-mighty Manchester United. It was Alex Ferguson's United, a team with Irwin and Stam at the back, Beckham and Scholes in midfield, and the irrepressible pairing of Cole and Yorke up front. They were reigning Premier League champions, and would go on to retain their crown a few months later. They didn't lose too often, and they certainly didn't get battered into submission on many occasions.

Now that I was living in Woodford, on the far end of the eastbound Central Line in terms of London's transport system, it was a far cry from the days when I could walk from home to Stamford Bridge and back. I also had a heavily-pregnant wife – Lisa was due to deliver what would be our final little package on October 11th, and there had been plenty of indications that the baby might arrive sooner.

When the new season's fixtures were published every June, United at home was always one that I and no doubt the vast majority of others looked for. I had spotted that it might be inconveniently scheduled, but as long as I kept my phone on and could jump on a train home at the first sign of movement, all would be fine. I checked with Lisa and she was comfortable with that.

The problem arose when one day in the week before the United game, as I was coming home from work I spotted a poster which said there would be no Central Line service that weekend out towards the east, due to planned maintenance works. Thanks, guys.

I didn't need to ask and I didn't need to be told, I knew that if I went to the game it could take me anything between two to three hours to get there, and the same to get back. With a couple of hours spent in and around Stamford Bridge between journeys, I was potentially out of the house for eight hours. There was no way I was going to risk missing the birth, and this was a significant risk.

As many of you will already have realised, on October 3rd 1999 Chelsea beat Manchester United 5-0. I watched it live on TV and it was so exciting, I nearly gave birth myself. Five days later, Sam Matthew Barker showed his handsome face for the first time, although he didn't immediately look handsome. In fact, he looked like a doorman, and he had penetrating eyes that kept following me around the delivery suite. I would have told him off for intimidating me if I hadn't felt so intimidated by him. But he arrived quickly, roughly three hours from start to finish, and had that happened five days earlier, I would never have got back in time to see it. Some things are more important than football, they're just few and far between.

SATURDAY 4TH MAY 2002

FA Cup Final

Arsenal 2 Chelsea 0

Ten years after Sunderland had broken my heart with their devastating late FA Cup win at Roker Park, I was reunited with my travel partner from that night, Steve McNally, for the 2002 Final against Arsenal in Cardiff. Steve had relocated to Yorkshire through work in the mid-90s, and I had seen far less of him as a result. However, when our old friend Dean Dennis got hitched in New Zealand and threw a subsequent wedding party back in London in April 2002, I had the pleasure of catching up properly with him again. Not surprisingly, the conversation quickly turned to merciless banter at other people's expense, and numerous largely unprintable stories being recounted, followed by hysterical laughter and the occasional 'how on earth did we get away with that?' head shake.

The Blues had recently beaten Fulham in a semi-final at Villa Park, securing their place in the showpiece final against Arsenal, who were seeking a Premier League and FA Cup double that year. With Wembley being redeveloped, this would be the second year that Cardiff had hosted the final. The Gunners had also played in the previous season's game, where they were beaten by Liverpool. On the night of Dean's party, Steve and I vowed that we would do everything in our power to get our hands on tickets together for the game. Thankfully, a lady at my work had connections with the FA and was able to get us two tickets in the 'mixed zone' along one side of the pitch. The mixed zone sounded interesting – neither Steve nor I were ever inclined to hide our colours, so to speak, although we did have the sense to be mildly respectful one night at West Ham when four of us sat in the Bobby Moore Stand. However, Arsenal supporters are a different prospect to those naughty East London Irons, and this was the FA Cup Final. It would help if the mixed zone was largely blue, but it wouldn't be the end of the world if it wasn't!

Steve and I booked a return coach from Victoria to Cardiff, and when we took our seats we quickly discovered that we were the only Chelsea supporters on it. I suppose it's possible there may have been one or two who realised they were massively outnumbered and just kept their heads down, but we were certainly the only ones who had any intention of reminding the Gooners on-board of their place in London's league of fans. Big club, yes. Joke support – an even bigger yes.

I think the journey to Cardiff was less fun for the majority of that bus than for the tiny minority in two seats near the back, but it was genuinely good natured banter. Steve and I were in schoolboy mode, two blokes acting the goat and just ripping it out of the Arsenal fans without any real malice. There were even some friendly goodbyes shared when we disembarked in the Welsh capital. And we tipped the driver a bit on top, to thank him for tolerating us.

Meeting up with other Chelsea mates, we had a few drinks in Queen Street to ensure we wouldn't suddenly grow up. At this point I would like to thank the Chelsea fans who were paying for drinks with moody tenners. I got lumbered with a couple and had no idea until I tried to use one in a local shop the following day. Anyway, suffice to say Steve and I were deep in schoolboy mode by the time we reached the stadium, handed over our tickets, found our gate and landed in the mixed zone. A very, very red and white mixed zone I might add. Still, needs must...

Within minutes of the game kicking off, Steve and I had our very own member of the Heddlu Constabulary assigned to us. Have you seen the size of the coppers in Cardiff? They're massive. So are the ones in Caerdydd apparently, which gets a mention on all the road signs down that way, although I don't think I've ever been there. Anyway, this one definitely posed a bigger threat to us than every Arsenal supporter at that game combined. Although that's not really true, because unlike many other police forces, the guys in Cardiff seem to know the difference between a trouble-maker and a piss-taker. Steve and I were definitely in the latter category, and we ended up having a laugh throughout the first-half with our new mate, before he disappeared at half-time safe in the knowledge that all the Arsenal fans in the mixed zone were safe from harm.

Sadly for us, Chelsea succumbed to two second-half goals and Arsenal lifted the trophy. I was a bit tipsy but not too drunk to see that the referee, Mike Riley, practically handed the game to them right from the start. I was pleased to see so many newspaper reports the following day making reference to Riley's seemingly red-tinted performance. Unfortunately, even in 2022 that man continues to bring his incompetence to bear on English football.

When we left the ground and headed back to the meeting point for the bus, Steve and I were expecting an irritating journey home, surrounded by smug Arsenal fans with a double to celebrate. However, before we reached the meeting point we stumbled across our bus parked in a random street. It was just as well because we were running late and risked missing it. As we jumped on board, we asked the driver why he was parked here. He explained that the coaches had been told to relocate from the normal place. He didn't seem too concerned though, telling us to climb on and take our seats. It was only then that we realised we were the first ones back on the coach. So imagine our surprise when we took our seats, felt the engine start, and heard the driver say "I'm not waiting for the others." Proper Chels. And that set us off laughing again.

Steve went back up north and we kept in touch primarily on Facebook. Then, one Saturday evening in February 2011 I received a text from him out of the blue, asking if I was going to the following day's Chelsea game. We had just signed Fernando Torres from Liverpool, and he would be making his debut against the Reds at Stamford Bridge on Sunday. "Yes mate, why?" "I'm going, fancy meeting up? I think it'll be my last game." "What do you mean your last game?" "Well, I've been diagnosed with Motor Neurone Disease and basically I'm fucked."

My blood ran cold, even more so when I researched the condition and got a better understanding of the gravity of Steve's situation. I was numb. I'd been speaking to him via Facebook without knowing he'd had this diagnosis, or that he was even unwell. I met up with him and a few others the following day and could see how he shook. His brother, Andrew, helped Steve hold his drink otherwise it would spill. Steve told me he'd taken the decision to stop going to football after the last Chelsea game he'd been to, as he'd fallen outside Fulham Broadway and been verbally abused by a policeman who accused him of being drunk. This charming copper had refused to listen when Steve tried to explain his condition. And they wonder why they get a bad reputation.

As luck would have it, we discovered that Steve and I were both working locally to each other at that time, Steve in Abbey Wood and myself in Woolwich. A few weeks later I went over to Steve's work on Friday evening for a function, but it was painful to see the level of support he required. Fortunately, his wife-to-be, Valda, worked with him and provided the support.

Steve and Valda got married in December 2013 and they kindly invited my family and I. His best man was Stacey Houghton, another familiar Chelsea face and one of those we met up with in Cardiff in 2002. He and Steve had been friends since their school days. Steve was unable to deliver his speech himself, but when Stacey and I got a light-hearted mention in it – another of those 'how did we get away with that?'

stories – I didn't know whether to laugh or cry.

Steve McNally passed away in October 2017, aged 44. He is, and always will be, much missed.

SATURDAY 19TH MAY 2007

FA Cup Final

Chelsea 1 Manchester United 0

Having played in and won the last FA Cup Final at the original Wembley, seven years prior, Chelsea reached another Final in 2007, which would be the first played at the redeveloped national stadium. Their opponents would be Manchester United, the two best teams in the country meeting in what, for Chelsea, would be significant compensation for losing their Premier League crown to United, if they could secure a win in the showpiece match.

The Wembley rebuild project had been late finishing, and had run an eye-watering £462,000,000 over its original estimated budget. FOUR HUNDRED AND SIXTY TWO MILLION POUNDS. Even for a project with as incompetent an organisation as the Football Association at its helm, this was an astonishing cost overrun. Of course, somebody had to pay, and it wasn't going to be that organisation's overpaid and overfed board of directors. No, it was going to be Wembley's customers and consumers.

In the run-up to the Final, there was much talk about the inflated ticket prices. It hadn't bypassed many media outlets that the cheapest-priced ticket had been greedily hiked up fully 40% on what had been charged just a year earlier, so the tone had been set by the FA from the outset. We were going to pay for their monumental incompetence. Then, as the day approached, the price list for food and drink was leaked to the media, and the stated prices were scandalous. Supporters groups from both United and Chelsea galvanised themselves in a joint attempt at either forcing the FA to revisit their pricing policy or, should this fail, to encourage supporters attending the game to boycott the food and drink outlets inside the national stadium. My good friend David Johnstone, one of Stamford Bridge's most familiar matchday faces and editor of the highly-regarded CFCUK fanzine, asked if I would take the role of spokesperson for the Chelsea supporters groups. I was initially nervous and reluctant to agree, but eventually said I'd do it largely because David needed somebody he trusted to carry out the role, and I owed him numerous favours for all the support he had given me when I was writing *Celery!*

My first media assignment came six days before the Final, when I spoke to a BBC local news team in Fulham Road after the last game of the Premier League season at home to Everton. I'd done my research, had the facts and the points I needed to make rehearsed in my head, and as a result I think it went OK. I can't say I wanted to be on camera, but I wasn't too fazed by the experience.

As I recall it, the rest of that week remained quiet until Friday, the day before the match. Suddenly, half of London seemed to want a few minutes with me. I hadn't been this popular since… well, since the day I was born. Starting early with a car collecting me from home and whisking me to and from the studio from which the BBC Asia network transmitted, I was literally on the go all day. I was supposed to be working, but quickly realised my phone was going to be ringing off the hook that day, so had to take an impromptu day off.

No sooner had I been returned home by my BBC driver, than Sky News got in touch to ask if I would be happy to go to their Westminster studio to be interviewed. I made my way over there, into the offices and into make-up, then into a studio to be grilled – unlike tomorrow's £10 Wembley burgers, which would probably be microwaved. The Sky News guy tried to keep it lighthearted but was a bit full of himself. I just concentrated on making my key points and not being distracted by the fact that he may have thought this was a non-story. I was getting the hang of this.

On conclusion of the Sky News interview, I was asked if I could stay where I was so that I could be linked to Sky Sports News, as they would like to speak to me too. Sure enough, after just a few minutes the familiar surroundings and faces of two Sky Sports News presenters appeared before me, and I was going live to a programme I regularly watched. It was all quite surreal.

Having met a couple of Sky Sports News presenters, Rob Wotton (Chelsea) and Tony Wrighton (QPR), I had realised that these guys were genuine football people, proper supporters of their teams, and it was therefore no surprise to me that in my interview with their channel, the matter at hand was taken far more seriously than by their news colleagues.

Having spent a whirlwind hour or so in the Sky studio, I was just about to leave when a lady called after me to tell me I still had a face full of make-up! In my slightly flustered state, wondering who and how many people had left messages for me while I had been on-air, I was about to walk out into a packed Central London looking like Boy George's fat sibling. I will always be indebted to that lady who called me back and cleaned my face.

As I recall, I had only one message I needed to respond to once I'd finished with Sky, and that was from BBC London News, saying they would like to do a piece with me and would call again. I jumped on a train back to Woodford and was just putting the key in my front door when my phone rang again, and it was BBC reporter Karl Mercer. He asked if I was still in Central London and I told him I wasn't. He then asked if there was any chance I and a few friends could go back there for a five-a-side kick about with some United fans, but this one I knew I had to decline. There was no way I was heading back into town, and I couldn't realistically gather a team of friends at such short notice when most were at work. Karl was very understanding and said perhaps another time. He seemed a very decent guy, and I wished I'd been able to help him out but it just wasn't logistically possible.

That evening I did a couple of radio interviews, and my job as spokesperson was done. Tomorrow was Cup Final day, and other than not buying from any of the kiosks – something I've continued to resist doing at Wembley ever since – my only interest for the next 24 hours was the ninety minutes of football that would determine whether the famous old trophy would head to the naughty north or the sexy south.

Before heading over to Wembley on the day of the Final, I met up with Cliff Auger and a few of his friends for a drink and a bit of a de-brief on the previous day's events. Cliff is well known at Chelsea, and is at the heart of many of the supporters' initiatives to help others, including the annual Stamford Bridge sleepout to raise money for homeless charities, and the matchday food bank collections he co-ordinates before kick-off in Fulham Road. As I left the pub to make my way to Wembley, I grabbed a sandwich from a local shop and as I walked down the road with it, somebody shouted "Oi, mate. I hope you didn't buy that at Wembley."

The 2007 FA Cup Final was a surprisingly poor affair, unbecoming of two such talented sides and the occasion itself. The first FA Cup Final under the arch did not match up to many played previously in the shadow of the twin towers. Nevertheless, in these fixtures the result is all-important, so when Didier Drogba scored the only goal of the game in the dying minutes of extra-time, the blue half of the stadium celebrated wildly, while the red half sulked. United had been crowned Premier League champions for the first time in four years just a fortnight earlier, but that fact clearly didn't make a lot of difference in the immediate aftermath of Drogba's goal and the final whistle. One end of the ground was deflated, the other jubilant. Winning the first Cup Final at the 'new' Wembley was as historic as winning the last one at its previous incarnation. Chelsea had done both. And the cherry on the icing on the cake came when we were told that revenue from food and drinks kiosks at the 2007 game were significantly lower than had been projected by Wembley Stadium. A successful day all round.

WEDNESDAY 21ST MAY 2007

UEFA Champions League Final
Chelsea 1 Manchester United 1
(United won 6-5 on penalties)

Almost a year to the day since Chelsea had triumphed over Manchester United in the 2007 FA Cup Final, the sides met again for an even bigger prize. It had always felt likely once Roman Abramovich had bought Chelsea Football Club that the Blues would soon find themselves in this position, but when Liverpool were beaten in a tense semi-final at the Bridge, it still seemed surreal that we would be going to Moscow for the 2008 showpiece Final.

This outcome had seemed highly unlikely earlier in the campaign, when after a tepid start to their Premier League campaign, Chelsea struggled to a 1-1 draw at home to Norwegian side Rosenborg in their first Champions League group game. I was there on a corporate ticket courtesy of a friend of mine, Warren Hackett, who as a former pro footballer himself sensed that all was not well in the ranks. Before the game, as we were having our pre-match meal, we witnessed the sight of Chelsea's owner being hastily sped through the lounge surrounded by a group of burly security men. Anybody who had got in their way would have known all about it – it was like one of those old Roadrunner cartoons of my childhood, all that was missing was a huge puff of dust. It was a strange thing to observe, somewhat akin to a president or member of a royal family being protected from the public as they move from one place to another. I remember thinking that I wouldn't fancy living my life that way, regardless of the financial reward.

Two days after that Rosenborg game, and following months of speculation about disagreements between Jose Mourinho and other club personnel, the manager was gone. His final game had been played out in front of a half-empty stadium, as the Chelsea board opted to increase the ticket prices for largely routine Champions League group games. That decision backfired as the supporters voted with their feet – I would have done the same had the corporate freebie not been offered to me – but it led to a really dismal night, and an unfitting end to Mourinho's scintillating but often divisive first spell at the club.

With the little-known Israeli Avram Grant in the managerial hot-seat, the 2007/08 season proved to be an intriguing one. Chelsea remained competitive in all competitions, but things on the pitch never felt quite as secure as they had in the seasons immediately prior. Within weeks of taking charge, Grant oversaw a huge 6-0 victory against Manchester City which had the fans purring at the quality of the football on show. However, Chelsea reached the Final of the League Cup but surrendered a lead as they were overcome at Wembley by the old enemy, Tottenham Hotspur. The Blues were strong favourites to retain the FA Cup, as many of the big clubs fell by the wayside early, but an atrocious defeat at Barnsley in the fifth round put paid to that idea. Both of these results were unthinkable under Mourinho. However, Grant's team continued to thrive in the Champions League, aided in part by a fortunate draw which saw them play both Olympiacos of Greece and Turkey's Fenerbahçe in the knockout stage, ahead of the semi-final clash with perennial irritants Liverpool.

Having been beaten at the same stage in two of Mourinho's three seasons in charge, it was highly ironic that third time lucky came on the less likely – but eminently more likeable – Grant's watch (Chelsea would go on to defeat Liverpool again in the quarter-finals of the following season's competition, before losing on away goals to Barcelona in the last-four in what can generously be described as 'highly dubious' circumstances). On a night when Stamford Bridge was crackling with passion, a trip to Moscow was secured with a 3-2 win after extra-time, following a 1-1 draw at Anfield in the first leg. It is a night made famous by the poignant image of Frank Lampard, just days after his mother, Pat, had passed away, dropping to his knees in tears after scoring a penalty to put Chelsea ahead in the tie. He wasn't the only man in blue that night who was moved to tears by that moment.

In the days prior to the Final, Mark Worrall, David Johnstone and I did a piece for BBC TV with Chris Hollins, son of John and at the time a BBC presenter, and three Manchester United fans in a Russian hotel in Bayswater. Strangely, it coincided with the annual League Managers Awards dinner nearby, and I ended up walking through Bayswater chatting to former Spurs manager and Chelsea assistant boss, Peter Shreeves. What a nice bloke he is.

The BBC piece was fun to be a part of, and the United fans were all decent guys (spoiler alert: one of them texted me the day after the Final to say we didn't deserve to lose the game in the way we did), as was Hollins himself, who not only shares his father's looks but also his ebullient personality. We were there to discuss the game while sampling traditional Russian food, and for the first time in my life I ate caviar.

There won't be a second time.

I travelled to Moscow on a day trip with my friends Roland Birch, Dominic Dennis (like his namesake Dean, a pal from my film company days) and Dominic's dad, Alan. There were a lot of years watching Chelsea through thick and thin amongst the four of us, and none of us were going to miss this occasion. Unfortunately, the weather wasn't kind and an already bleak city looked even less attractive in the pouring rain. As in 1994 at Wembley, it seemed Manchester had brought the weather with them. It rained all day and all evening.

Moscow as a city didn't really appeal to me and I certainly wouldn't go back. The people looked miserable – probably not unlike Londoners on our daily commute if I'm honest – and the buildings other than in Red Square were as grey and dour as the people and the weather. I was particularly perturbed to see a black guy stopped by a couple of locals and asked if they could have a photo with him. He was very obliging, but I was a bit shocked to see a black person considered a novelty in 21st century Europe. The underground stations, however, were spectacular. I could hardly believe that they were lit by ornate chandeliers, the like of which wouldn't last five minutes in a London tube station.

Inside the ground it was apparent that a lot of the supporters in our end were Russians. United's support was loud and it was obvious throughout the day that there were more of them who had made the journey than us. Considering that both clubs' core fan base is in London and the Home Counties, I was a little disappointed by that. However, there was one fine moment in our end before kick-off, when everybody joined in with a song targeted at Liverpool supporters who constantly refer to their club's history and Chelsea's apparent lack of (yes, I know, they're a bit dim): "F*ck your history, we're here in Moscow." reverberated around the ground as the red half of Merseyside, the beaten semi-finalists, watched on their black and white TVs. Stolen from Radio Rentals in 1973.

For a neutral, the game must have been a pulsating watch. From memory, because I've never watched it back, United were largely dominant in the first period and Chelsea were in the ascendancy from thereon. Cristiano Ronaldo gave the Reds the lead before Lampard levelled matters just before half-time. We hit the woodwork three times after that, and Joe Cole was clearly fouled by Rio Ferdinand as he ran through on goal, but the UEFA officials chose to look the other way. Perhaps the turning point was Didier Drogba's sending off, which was not well received in our end as his petulance was always likely to be costly. That said, if pretty-boy Carlos Tevez hadn't coerced his willing team-mates into breaking with convention after one of our players had kicked the ball out so that an injured United player could get treatment, there would have been no need for the contretemps that followed. But that's Carlos Tevez, he is what he is.

As we all now know, because I gave the game away in an earlier paragraph, we lost the match in the cruellest way possible: on penalties. John Terry had a kick to win us the trophy – an opportunity which would have fallen on Drogba's broad shoulders had he still been on the pitch – but our legendary skipper slipped as he struck the ball, and his shot flew wide off the outside of a post. I watched that kick while the supporter in front of me turned and faced us in the row behind. When I said "He's f*cking missed it" I think we both knew where the cup with the big ears was heading.

The journey home was a grim one, the bunfight to get on an aeroplane would have been comical had we not all been very tired and very, very emotional. However, it was nice to see some of the Chelsea old boys in the airport, having been kindly flown out to the game courtesy of Roman Abramovich. As I said to John Bumstead: "I don't suppose we would ever have imagined being one kick away from winning the European Cup back in the old days."

When I got back to Stansted I gave Lisa a call, as I'd not been able to call her at all the previous day. It was now around 8am and she was getting ready for work. I made some small talk about landing safely and would be home soon, and then she asked how I was feeling. That was where the conversation ended. It would have all gone the way of Sunderland in 92 if I'd tried to answer her perfectly reasonable question.

As a postscript to this chapter, Roland Birch would very sadly contract cancer a couple of years after this. A season-ticket holder in the Shed with his wife and two daughters, we became friends as he lived locally and one of his daughters was in the same primary school class as Poppy. We often did the journey to and from games together, and he was good company. When Chelsea played Manchester City in the 2013 FA Cup semi-final at Wembley, I did a piece for Radio Five Live with David Johnstone and gave a shout out on air to Roland, who I knew had been hoping to be at the game but simply wasn't well enough. He passed away a few weeks later.

SATURDAY 27TH MARCH 2010

Premier League

Chelsea 7 Aston Villa 1

I don't know how things work at other big clubs, but the days of Chelsea players all convening to the Stamford Bridge players' bar at 5pm on a Saturday are very much a thing of the past. The Chelsea Health Club is where it's at now.

During Carlo Ancelotti's magnificent first season at the helm, in which his team secured Chelsea's first and, to date, only domestic League and FA Cup double, Sam and I were very fortunate to be invited by David Johnstone to join him and a few others in the Health Club for post-match drinks. The first occasion was following a 2-0 win over Stoke City in the FA Cup, and the following weekend we repeated the experience after a 4-1 trouncing of Gianfranco Zola's West Ham. A week earlier I'd had no interest in whether any members of the Stoke party would make an appearance in the Club, but this was different. The little magician in charge of the Hammers was one of Chelsea's greatest ever players, and a great man too. After the Stoke game it was all about shaking hands with and having a quick chat to John Terry, Frank Lampard, Ashley Cole and his namesake Joe, who might just be the nicest man in football*. Now, it was just as much about getting a photo with and a handshake from the opposition manager. And sure enough, he didn't disappoint. Despite enduring a torrid afternoon which pushed his side closer to the Premier League's relegation zone, Zola arrived with his trademark smile and was friendly and gracious to everyone. Likewise, his assistant Kevin Hitchcock was warm and friendly despite his beloved team's defeat.

A fortnight later, Chelsea played Aston Villa at the Bridge. The fight for the Title was now a three-horse race between the Blues, Manchester United and Arsenal. On the day of the Villa game, United trounced Bolton, but the Gunners dropped points in typical style by surrendering victory in the last minute at Birmingham. However, it was Chelsea's result that really caught the eye. Villa, who a fortnight later would be swept aside 3-0 by the Blues in an FA Cup semi-final at Wembley, were destroyed 7-1 by a ruthless display of all-round power and lethal finishing which typified Ancelotti's team that season. Throughout that campaign, Chelsea scored seven on three occasions and sealed the Premier

League crown on the final day by putting eight past Wigan Athletic.

Frank Lampard scored four of Chelsea's seven that day, and when he walked into the Health Club after the game with a couple of friends, those of us around our table gave him a round of applause. Frank humbly asked us to stop because he was embarrassed, but stayed with us for a chat. While he was talking, he was stood right behind me and was rubbing my shoulders. I had no idea why, and at another time in another place, had a man helped himself to this I suspect it wouldn't have ended well, but this was Frank Lampard. Frank Lampard massaging my shoulders. Who was I to complain?

Before we left, another surprise arrived in the shape of Didier Drogba, who's appearance we hadn't anticipated. Sam's little face lit up, he was so pleased to see his favourite player. I have a photo in my wallet of my then ten-year-old son beaming alongside Didier, which makes me smile every time I look at it.

That was a great season, with many highlights. When the Double was clinched at Wembley, with a Cup Final win over Portsmouth, I was so proud of what Chelsea had achieved that I took to social media with a slightly over-emotional post about how my wonderful club had made an old man very happy. And despite an impromptu massage that made a grown man smile more than it perhaps should have, I'm pleased to say that the Blues securing their first domestic double was the only happy ending to report.

*When I went on holiday to Tampa with my family in 2017, I asked David Johnstone to ask Joe Cole, who at the time was playing for Tampa Bay Rowdies, if he would fancy meeting up with my Chelsea-mad sons and I while we were there. He said yes and passed on his number, and on the penultimate day of what was a great holiday, Dan, Sam and I met him at the Rowdies Stadium to watch a training session and go for a post-session coffee. In what was a fantastic holiday where loads of great memories were made, that day was right up there with the very best of them.

SATURDAY 19TH MAY 2012

UEFA Champions League Final
Bayern Munich 1 Chelsea 1
(Chelsea won 4-3 on penalties)

Before I describe this as the greatest night of my life, let's remove the elephant in the room. Many people will say that getting married and/or seeing their children born was the greatest day of their life. I get that. But there's a difference. In my eyes, there are things that are important in the grand scheme, and others which probably aren't. I could have lived a perfectly happy life without seeing Chelsea win the Champions League, but my life would never have been this happy without Lisa and my children in it. I was very emotional when the Blues did the business in Munich, but I kept the tears at bay. Just. I cried like a baby myself when all three of my kids showed their faces for the first time. Those personal days are the most overwhelming, the most emotional and, without a shadow of a doubt, the most important. But that night in Munich, in the context of something that perhaps isn't so important in the grand scheme but is like a carnal desire that you dream of fulfilling, was absolutely bloody fantastic. The greatest.

As with the previous Final, in 2008, this one came at the end of a tempestuous domestic campaign during which a Portuguese boss was fired. This manager, however, had neither the charm nor the credentials of his predecessor. Andre Villas-Boas was a smartarse appointment that backfired on a Chelsea board who saw fit to ruthlessly dispense with Carlo Ancelotti in order to accommodate him. Fortunately, Roberto di Matteo was Villas-Boas' right-hand man in the Stamford Bridge dugout, and he would eventually steer the club back in the right direction in the final weeks of the season.

Villas-Boas oversaw a solid if unspectacular start to the season, but when things started to go awry from autumn onwards, he was powerless to react. His naïve defensive set-up was exposed horribly in a 5-3 home defeat by Arsenal, but the belligerent boss persisted with his own preferred methods and subsequently saw what was once fortress Stamford Bridge, become a playground for opponents as Liverpool (twice) and Aston Villa both won there before the end of the year, and even lowly neighbours Fulham managed a draw. In February, on the same pitch, Chelsea squandered a 3-0 lead to draw 3-3 with Howard Webb's Manchester United side, and a fortnight later had to rely on a second-half equaliser to retain an interest in the FA Cup, managing just a draw at home to second-flight Birmingham City. Three days after that dismal display, a 3-1 beating in Naples left Chelsea's Champions League aspirations hanging by a thread for another season.

On the first weekend in March, with a Cup replay at Birmingham and a home second leg against Napoli on the horizon, Chelsea were beaten by West Bromwich Albion. Tradition dictates these days that a defeat at The Hawthorns usually precedes a Stamford Bridge managerial casualty, and so it proved with future Tottenham Hotspur manager Villas-Boas (I mention the Spurs post to demonstrate just how quickly his career fell into decline once he left Chelsea). To the relief of the Stamford Bridge faithful, the Portuguese was shown the door and his assistant, the club's legendary former midfielder di Matteo, put in temporary charge of the team. Not surprisingly, the improvement in mood and performance was instant. The replay at Birmingham was comfortably navigated, before Stoke City were beaten at the Bridge. An astonishing game saw Chelsea overcome Napoli 4-1 after extra-time to seal their place in the quarter-finals of the Champions League, and a 5-2 thrashing of Leicester City sent the Blues into the last four of the FA Cup. We didn't know it at the time, but the scene had been set for a sensational final few weeks of the season.

Chelsea were drawn to play Benfica in the Champions League, and stole a 1-0 win away from home in the first leg. For the return I sat with Mickey Thomas courtesy of tickets arranged by Brian Rowan, a well-known face around Stamford Bridge. Brian had also sorted a pair of tickets for Andrew Wood, known to all as Woody, a Chelsea supporter from Mansfield who I had only previously 'met' on Twitter, where his sense of humour had made him a very popular member of the Chelsea 'Twitterati'. This was the first time we had actually met, and he was no less funny in person. Within seconds he was pulling fake ten pound notes out of his pocket to give to Mickey.

Benfica were beaten 2-1 that night, to set up a semi-final clash with Barcelona. Before that, there was the small matter of an FA Cup semi against Spurs at Wembley. Either Woody or I, I can't remember which, had a spare ticket for the game, so we went together and had a great laugh. I mean, you would have a great laugh when your team is trampling all over Spurs – unusually, many people's favourites for that game due to their strong recent form – to the extent that the only people left in their half of the stadium at full-time were their players and Chas and Dave.

Chelsea 5 Tottenham Hotspur 1. Back at Wembley in May, now for Barcelona.

Robbie di Matteo, as we all now know, was not the long-term answer for Chelsea, but in the final few Champions League games that season, he offered a very Italian, managerial masterclass built on organisation and defence. The first leg against Barcelona, at the Bridge, was one of the most defensive displays you will ever see from a home side with no lead to protect. There were times when we seemed to be flying by the seat of our pants, but the tactical ploy paid off and a 1-0 victory, courtesy of Didier Drogba's finish from a swift counter-attack, was vindication for the way di Matteo had set his side up.

The second leg, in the Nou Camp, was incredible and is one game I would have given my right arm to witness live. I think my neighbours might have wished I had too, because the noise I made when Fernando Torres skipped around Victor Valdes and nudged the ball into an empty net to send Chelsea to the Final was as loud as it was stupid. It was just a noise, there were no actual words. The fact that the Blues had overcome Barcelona on their own pitch, with just ten men after John Terry was sent off in the first period, and from two goals down, was testament to the timing of Villas-Boas' replacement. This was not possible under him – Robbie had the magic touch as a manager, matching what he had as a player a decade and a half previously.

A week before the Champions League Final, there was the FA Cup Final to contest with Liverpool. There is a real enmity between the supporters of both clubs nowadays, a spiteful animosity fuelled by the antics of Jose Mourinho and Rafael Benitez throughout the period when the two clubs were constantly being pitched against each other in the Champions League. There had been some booing of a minute silence to respect the victims of the Hillsborough tragedy before the Cup clash with Spurs at Wembley, and that was still fresh in some people's minds on Cup Final day. I'm not sure if people were booing the FA for refusing to switch the dates of the semi-finals so that Chelsea didn't have to play Spurs two days before taking on Barcelona, or if they were booing Liverpool for continuing a long-held tradition of not playing on 15th April, the anniversary of the Hillsborough tragedy. As unpalatable as the reaction was, I'd at least like to think it was aimed at the FA for simply not allowing Chelsea's game with Spurs to be rescheduled to a more suitable date. Although I'm certainly no fan of Liverpool Football Club, I have nothing but respect for the fact that they keep that date a sacred one in the calendar.

As I'm not a fan of Liverpool Football Club, I can't explain why their supporters chose to boo their own national anthem before kick-off. It did make me laugh though. It was utterly bizarre. And I think it probably did rattle many of my fellow Chelsea supporters, but I simply found it hilarious.

The dumbing down of the FA Cup by the very same organisation it's named after was never more evident to me than on that day. An early evening kick-off on a day when there was a full programme of League fixtures told us all we needed to know about the current status of the trophy. Where Cup Final day used to be just that – an all-day affair – it is now tucked away in an evening slot, the TV rights sold to some money-grabbing channel, and if your club is from north of Birmingham and you want to be at the game, you'd best forget all about getting home on a train that night. There'll be none running by the time the game's over.

Chelsea won the 2012 Final 2-1, thanks to goals from Ramires and, of course, Drogba. Roberto di Matteo had his first managerial trophy with the Blues, and now thoughts could turn to Munich.

I travelled to Bavaria with Paul Ramsay, who I'd also been with on the memorable day 15 years earlier, when the FA Cup meant something and we saw Chelsea clinch it with a win over Middlesbrough. Even then, despite all the investment in continental talent, we would never have believed that one day we would be heading off together to a Champions League Final. We'd booked our flights as soon as the semi-final was over, but match tickets were going to be harder to come by. For a while we had the promise of one, courtesy again of the ever-reliable Brian Rowan, but then Mickey Thomas came up trumps through the most unlikely of routes: Manchester United had some and one of the ladies he knew at Old Trafford had a contact at Chelsea, so she sent them to Stamford Bridge and we sent about £660 the other way. They were expensive tickets but we would have paid far more if necessary, especially if we'd possessed some hindsight. I think Paul would agree that it's the best £660 we ever spent. And we had Peter Kenyon sitting directly behind us, so we knew we were in the posh seats.

We flew out early on the Herbert's Express from Gatwick. Fortunately, Paul lives not far from the airport and was able to get us there quickly. It was just as well, as our check-in was around 4am if I remember correctly. Once all the Herberts had disembarked, we jumped on a train and headed towards the Marienplatz. Despite our early arrival, it was already busy outside the famous (and beautiful) cathedral, and the weather was fantastic. I don't think either of us were overly-optimistic of a win, especially as John Terry, Raul Meireles, Branislav Ivanovic and Ramires were all suspended, and centre-halves David Luiz and Gary Cahill both playing on one leg, but we had to be there all the same. Of course, the fact that Bayern Munich were the other finalists, playing in their own stadium, was a bit of a hindrance too.

We didn't stray far from the Marienplatz all day, just wandered around in the sunshine and stopped for food and drink when necessary. The atmosphere was fine, there was no hint of any trouble that we saw, and the English and German supporters mingled happily for the most part. It was a bit like that Christmas Day football match during World War One. Maybe Paul McCartney should write a song about it.

When it was time to head over to the Allianz Arena, Paul and I joined hundreds of others in squeezing onto a train that was dangerously overloaded with passengers. However, it was safer than staying on the platform which was also dangerously overloaded with passengers… and it was something of a miracle that nobody ended up in front of a train that day. Wouldn't happen on the London Underground (well, they'd probably be on strike. Safe as houses.).

Inside the ground I remember running into Graham Bush on the concourse. I love Bushers, he's a great guy and for a few years he was bass player for Madness. We were all hoping we would hear One Step Beyond after the final whistle.

We were actually in the ground much earlier than we needed to be, so we watched the stands fill up and we listened to some annoying bloke mingling and bantering with the fans at both ends of the stadium. By the time the teams came out, there was a real sense of tension in the air. Everybody wanted to hit the bloke with the mic.

I remember looking at the teams as they lined up on the pitch. Jose Bosingwa was in the side in place of Ivanovic. I'd never rated him from day one, although he did do a sterling job in the Nou Camp a few weeks ago. And Ryan Bertrand had been given a place in the team – his European debut. He was playing in front of Ashley Cole but was primarily a left-back himself, so this was another defensive move from di Matteo. It looked a bit of a gamble, but Bertrand turned in a solid if unspectacular performance. In fact, solid but unspectacular would be the order of the day. Or the evening, to be precise.

To be totally honest, I'm not sure I can really say I enjoyed the game. It was bit of a nail-biter with Bayern on top throughout, and it felt like our mixed bag of whoever was fit and had boots were clinging on grimly at times. We were also indebted to Bayern's striker, Mario Gomez, who turned in a performance reminiscent of Mark Falco during his ill-fated loan spell at the Bridge in 1982.

The game finally burst into life in the final ten minutes of normal time. First, with just seven minutes remaining, Bayern's Thomas Muller popped up at the far post to head past Petr Cech and send the home fans wild. At that point, the Cup was theirs. Muller certainly thought so, and when he was substituted a couple of minutes later he was positively ecstatic as he left the pitch and celebrated with his team-mates and the German supporters. But it was a man who had joined the action just seconds before Muller departed, Fernando Torres, who won a corner in the final minute. We all roared as Juan Mata ran across to take the kick, but I know that at that point I was largely resigned to witnessing another Champions League Final defeat. And then it happened... Mata's cross was immaculate and both Didier Drogba and Frank Lampard made a move towards the ball. As Drogba jumped with his marker, Jerome Boateng, he got a shove in the back which propelled him onto the ball and with the fiercest of headers he sent the ball past Manuel Neuer, the German stopper able to parry but not stop the ball as it made its way into the top of the net. Cue absolute bedlam where we were sitting – in what was supposed to be a mixed area – and especially behind the goal where Drogba had dispatched the ball. What a moment that was. Not just on the night but in my life. The adrenalin rush was ridiculous – a last-minute equaliser in the Champions League Final. Unbelievable.

Chelsea had one more chance to win the game before the whistle blew, and for the first time that night I was actually confident that we were going to win. We were awarded a free-kick in Drogba territory about 25 yards from goal. I thought, to quote Gary Neville, it was written in the stars. Unfortunately, it wasn't. Not that time anyway.

Extra-time wasn't dissimilar to the ninety minutes which had preceded it. Bayern looked generally more dangerous and more likely to win, and our boys at times looked dead on their feet. Even Drogba looked tired when he tripped Franck Ribery to concede a penalty early in the piece, but not for the last time that night, Petr Cech came to the rescue when he saved Arjen Robben's poorly struck shot. Oh, it was bedlam behind that goal again. And it was bedlam in the mixed seats too.

When the final whistle blew and we knew it was going to penalties, there seemed to be an inevitability about the outcome. I'd seen Chelsea lose plenty of penalty shootouts but couldn't remember too many wins. West Brom in the Full Members Cup... Ipswich in the Simod Cup, which was the same trophy but now with a sponsor... a Charity Shield against Manchester United. I could recall a small handful of happy outcomes, but it was a reach. And now we were about to go up against a bunch of Germans in their own stadium. I felt sick. And when Mata missed our first kick, I was fairly close to tears.

When Croatian striker Ivica Olic, who had been brought on from the bench potentially for this specific scenario, stepped up to take Bayern's fourth kick, there was little doubt that if he converted it would be game over. The home side would have a 4-2 lead, meaning they were guaranteed a kick to win the trophy, whereas Chelsea had to ensure their last two kicks were converted to stay alive. He struck it to Cech's left, but Big Pete had his number and threw himself across to claw it away. GAME. BACK. ON. Bedlam at our end. Bedlam. Ashley Cole stepped forward to strike a perfect pen past Neuer, and the score was 3-3 with both sides having missed one apiece. Bastian Schweinsteiger, Bayern's star man, and Didier Drogba, Chelsea's star striker, would be the men who were, literally, on the spot.

Schweinsteiger looked unusually nervous when he stepped forward. Like his goalkeeper, Neuer, he usually gave off an air of Teutonic arrogance which, also like Neuer, he generally backed up with his performances. On this evening, though, he didn't look quite so confident. He, like Olic, opted to go to Cech's left, but this time Big Pete got the faintest of touches – impossible to spot at the time – and sent the ball onto the post and away. BEDLAM. BEDLAM. BEDLAM.

As Didier Drogba strode intently forward from the halfway line, I decided I couldn't watch. I'd made that mistake in Moscow and, in my mind at least, had decided that if I'd looked away when John Terry stepped forward to take his penalty, it would have found the net. I wasn't going to make that same mistake again. Paul tried to spin me round but I was adamant – I would watch our supporters and take my cue from them.

I didn't know it at the time, but as I was mentally recalling the horror of Moscow, on Sky TV commentator Martin Tyler was also referring to that night and the ill-fated penalty shootout, specifically the fact that had he not been sent-off earlier in the game, Drogba would have been in an identical position that night to the one he found himself in right now. It was a good point well made. History would probably have been rewritten had Drogba taken that kick in Moscow, but now the ultimate big match player had the perfect opportunity for redemption. With hindsight, it was never in doubt.

I peeped over my right shoulder sporadically as Drogba approached the penalty spot, ball in hand, at little more than a snail's pace. He placed the ball carefully on the spot and then took a short stride back, and as I turned and firmly fixed my gaze on the Chelsea supporters massed behind the goal to my left, the last thought that went through my mind as the referee's whistle blew was that Drogba hadn't taken a run-up. 'WHAT IS HE DOING???'

A second later, an enormous roar pierced the Bavarian air and a mass of bodies hurtled in all directions. It was a wonderful moment. Sheer hysteria. All around me, people were hugging each other, falling over, crying, looking startled and, in a variety of ways all of which came naturally to them at that very moment, celebrating the realisation that little old Chelsea Football Club were CHAMPIONS OF EUROPE. I may not have cried that night, but as I write about it now, almost ten years later, I have tears in my eyes and goosebumps all over my body. I know that it's unlikely that I will ever have another moment like that in my life again. It was a feeling of pure ecstasy and it's not something that can be manufactured.

If there was a downside to the night, it was that although the trophy presentation took place in the stand we were in, we couldn't actually see it and had to rely on the giant screens to get a glimpse of John Terry and Frank Lampard lifting the Cup. That, of course, was followed by celebrations on the pitch and with the fans which in many ways reminded me of those which took place on the pitch at Wembley after the 1997 FA Cup Final.

Paul and I eventually left the ground and I immediately bumped into David Johnstone, diligently selling his CFCUK fanzine while being hugged and kissed by numerous passers-by. His face was beaming as much as mine was, and we had a bear-hug that said 'We did it!'. We also saw Jeremy Clarkson leaving the stadium, I'd heard he was a Chelsea supporter but this was the first time I'd seen him at a game. He definitely wasn't at Rotherham.

In jovial mood, we got on a train and set about reversing our journey from earlier in the day. We headed back to Marienplatz and then took the connecting train to the airport. After a while, the carriage quietened down as we approached the end of the line and the number of passengers in the carriage diminished. Paul dozed off while I sat grinning inanely, when I suddenly noticed that the station we had just stopped at was the penultimate stop on the line. And that the airport was at the opposite end of the line.

I stood up to look at the train map and, spotting my dilemma, a Bayern supporter came over to speak to me and confirmed my worst thoughts. He advised us that it would be quicker to get off at the last stop and find a taxi to take us to the airport. I thanked him and wished his team well for the following season's competition – which they would ultimately win – and Paul and I then went looking for a taxi which, thankfully, arrived pretty quickly.

When we were dropped off at the airport we were already about 45 minutes late for the flight, but we sprinted through the departure lounges of various terminals until we eventually reached the Herberts Terminal, and to our relief we saw some familiar faces waiting to check tickets. We got a bit of heckling as we got on the plane but I think it was largely good natured – if it wasn't, then those people need to get their act together. You'd just won the Champions League, lads. And anyway, there were a couple of other guys who turned up later than we did, which I have to confess I was quite relieved about.

Back at Gatwick, we picked up Paul's car and he kindly drove me to Waterloo. It was about 5am and the underground hadn't started running yet, so I grabbed a paper and waited until it cranked into gear. I got the first Jubilee Line train to Stratford and then the Central Line to Woodford, and as I approached my stop a young lady sitting opposite me asked if I was just getting back from Munich. I told her I was and she said she works at Chelsea, and was doing the same as the Club had taken all staff members on a paid trip to the game. It was a nice touch and I was glad she had told me.

When I got home the house was still quiet, and everybody was in bed. I laid down on a settee in the living room and put the TV on, naturally tuning into Sky Sports News. I guess it had been something like nine hours since Drogba had tucked his penalty past Neuer but only now did I get to actually see it for the first time. I can't lie, with the benefit of hindsight I wished I'd seen it play out live. But no regrets, there's still a part of me that believes he would have missed it if I'd watched!

A little while later, Lisa came down the stairs and found me prostrate on the settee. She smiled and said "Did you enjoy that?" "That was the best night of my life.", I said. "I know it was.", she replied.

And it was.

Tragically, Woody would pass away in 2020 following a sudden heart attack. He was just 33 years old. He was an enormously well-known and popular figure amongst the Chelsea support, and his death reached the national media after Cesar Azpilicueta sent a message of condolence. The Twitter hashtag #Woody33 circulated widely ahead of his funeral, which sadly had to be a low-key affair due to the pandemic and the rules around allowable numbers at such events. I watched live coverage on an online stream and my heart went out – as it still does – to his wife, Hayley, and his two young sons, Joe and Nicholas. God bless, Woody.

SATURDAY 26TH JANUARY 2014

FA Cup Round 4

Chelsea 1 Stoke City 0

It had been 35 years since my dad had last set foot in Stamford Bridge. Three and a half decades since supporterless QPR had routed Chelsea 3-1, as the Blues headed for their second relegation in five years. He'd remained a Chelsea supporter, but the health issues and financial constraints of upgrading into the seats meant I now happily took the baton from him. As the years went on I often wondered if he missed it. We had never stopped talking about the Blues, it was always the main topic of conversation, and my dad always watched games on the telly. However, one day during Chelsea's successful pursuit of the FA Cup in 2000, I asked my dad if he wanted me to get him a ticket for the fifth round match against Leicester City, but he said he really wasn't that keen.

I have no idea what changed in the intervening years, but during a casual conversation about Chelsea in early 2014, my dad happened to mention that he would like to go back. I knew my best chance of getting a ticket was in the FA Cup, where I could use Sam's membership to buy an adult-priced ticket. So with Sam's blessing and kind offer to give up his seat for Grandad, I got us two tickets together for the Cup clash with Stoke City on 26th January. I'd also helped out former Chelsea captain Ron Harris a few months earlier with something, and he'd said if he could ever reciprocate I should just call. I wouldn't normally have called the favour in, but this was too good to miss. I called Ron and explained the situation with my dad and the Stoke game, and asked if he might be around to just pop by after the game to say hello to him. Chopper gladly obliged.

The day and the game itself flew by, but it felt quite special to be able to take my dad to a game after the numerous matches he'd taken me to as a boy. By my way of thinking, had my dad not set me on this royal blue path, some of the happiest times I've ever had would never have happened. I actually might not have supported Chelsea. Worse than that, I might have supported QPR like so many of my school friends did. What a grim thought that is. Devastating. I definitely owed my dad for raising me the right way.

We watched the Stoke game together from the Matthew Harding Upper Stand, and my dad got to meet a few of my friends both before the game and once we were in the ground. He recognised the stadium and the different areas, and pointed out where the rickety old North Stand had been before it was condemned in the mid-1970s.

Chelsea won that game against Stoke 1-0. Ron Harris was as good as his word, and he popped down from the hotel where he works as part of Chelsea's corporate hospitality team, to have a chat with my dad. It was a good day, although by the time we'd got back to the station we'd heard that Chelsea had drawn champions-elect Manchester City away in the next round, so perhaps there would be no return to the Bridge any time soon. After all, in that 2013/14 season, Chelsea were just a small horse according to their manager.

Thankfully, my dad didn't wait another 35 years to go back to the Bridge. He was there for the eventful opening game of the 2015/16 season, when Swansea secured a 2-2 draw and Jose Mourinho secured a writ from a physio; and again the following season to see Burnley dispatched 3-0 during Antonio Conte's wonderful first season in charge.

SATURDAY 3RD OCTOBER 2015

Premier League

Chelsea 1 Southampton 3

An entirely unexpected benefit of writing and publishing my first book – *Celery!* – was that I got to meet and become friends with a wide and diverse group of people. I had for a long time been aware of the matchday bustle around the CFCUK fanzine stall, but never personally knew the people involved. For many years I either stuck with my own small group of friends or attended games on my own, and in more recent times had attended with one of my kids. I recognised many regular faces in the same way that people have told me they recognised me, but I was generally quite happy contained within my own little cabals or, when alone, to just keep my own counsel outside of the ninety minutes when I would blow off steam. That all changed once David Johnstone kindly allowed me to sell my book from his stall, and it's fair to say that he and I have become close friends and confidants over subsequent years. Everybody knows DJ and most people love him. I always refer to him as Chelsea's most famous non-famous supporter.

On any given matchday, weather permitting of course, huge numbers of Blues fans will flock to the stall to pick up the latest copy of the fanzine – it famously costs 'only a pound' – and to peruse the ever-widening catalogue of Gate 17 titles available. The other reason they go to the stall is to chat. Team selection, tactics, new signings, old signings, Spurs' latest humiliation, *Love Island*... no subject is off-limits except the last one. We're all grown-ups after all, at least when it suits us.

Alex Giannini was a regular at the stall on matchdays, after being introduced by Martin King, a bit of a celebrity in his own right as a writer of some outstanding books on Chelsea and terrace culture, who was a long-time friend of Alex. Alex was an actor and performer, and had been the lead singer of Coast to Coast, a group who featured on *Top of the Pops* in 1981 when they had two hit songs: Jump the Broomstick and Do the Hucklebuck. By the time I got to know him he was primarily a stage actor, and a very good one too. When *Batman Live* came to London and the O2 Arena in 2010, playing to huge audiences, Alex played both The Penguin and Commissioner Gordon. Lisa and I took Poppy and Sam to see the show and Alex very kindly arranged for us all to go backstage for photos with the cast. Poppy and Sam loved it, and I have a great and treasured photo with him in character as The Penguin.

In the early weeks of the 2015/16 season, I was contacted by Danish film maker Thomas Pallesen. Thomas is a Chelsea supporter who has made some quite high-profile short films about the Blues, and I was familiar with his name, so I was flattered when he asked if I would like to be a part of a forthcoming project. Obviously I was happy to do so. We arranged to meet on the morning of Chelsea's clash with Southampton on October 3rd. I didn't have a ticket for the game, which was a 5.30pm kick-off, so we arranged an early meet in order that I had enough time to get back home before kick-off.

After a quick catch-up with my good friend Mark Worrall at the stall, I wandered up to Stamford Bridge to meet Thomas and record my piece to camera. Inevitably after a few minutes we were asked to stop filming on the premises, so we made our way back onto Fulham Road to complete the filming away from those pesky Chelsea security staff. I then took Thomas to the stall to meet a few of the other familiar faces, including Steve Mabey who also contributed a piece to the film. Should you want to see the film, it can be found on YouTube and has the title *Chelsea – My Story*.

After saying my goodbyes, I headed home and was shocked when I approached the end of my journey and got a phone signal, to see a message from Mark saying Alex Giannini had died suddenly the night before. He had been performing on tour in Plymouth and was found dead in his room. He was 55 years old.

Mark and I attended Alex's wake in central London, and met his widow Jenny and their children/step-children. Jenny was the daughter of Sir Harry Secombe, and was steeped in the entertainment industry. Mark and I spoke to Alex's very pleasant stepson, who told us that Alex talked about us and his days out at Chelsea regularly. Sadly, Jenny also passed away a couple of years after Alex.

3rd October 2015 is a day I'll remember all my life, with hugely mixed emotions. I really enjoyed making that film with Thomas. I found it cathartic to be able to open up about what Chelsea Football Club mean to me, why the 1980s were so special, my feelings when I finally saw the Blues lift the FA Cup in 1997, and how I got away with describing THAT night in Munich as the greatest ever to my ever-faithful wife, Lisa. However, people often discover that film for the first time and send it to me, and not a single time goes by when I watch it and don't recall both the good and the bad of that day.

Alex Giannini 1960-2015.

Sadly, Martin King also passed away while I was writing this book. Martin's fantastic sense of humour lit up the Fulham Road when we were peddling our wares together before games. He was a big character and somebody you always wanted on your side. He is sadly missed.

SATURDAY 5TH NOVEMBER 2016

Premier League

Chelsea 5 Everton 0

It's no coincidence that my two favourite seasons, those which were played out from August 1983 to May 1985, coincide with the days when I was younger, life was simpler, and on a day-to-day basis my moods would be determined by Chelsea's last result. As I grew older, busier, more prone to cynicism and stress from the rigours of daily life, it was no longer all about football. A Chelsea win couldn't stop my children getting ill, couldn't help Lisa and I pay our bills and, as I discovered to my cost a few years ago, couldn't stop me succumbing to a nasty little anxiety condition which in recent years has impacted significantly on the number of Chelsea games and other social occasions I attend. As wonderful as those 1983/84 and 1984/85 seasons were, it's unquestionable that I enjoyed them all the more because I was young and carefree at the time. And when I looked in the mirror, I wasn't appalled by what I saw. I'd give my right arm to have some of that self-confidence permeate through me again. So it came as a huge shock to me that in my middle-age, very rarely now an away match attendee and no longer prone to excitable bouts of screaming and shouting that leave my vocal chords redundant for days following a big fixture, that a season came out of nowhere and smacked me right between the eyes. And that season was Antonio Conte's first as manager. His second is best forgotten.

Having finished tenth in the Premier League the season before, with the toxic Jose Mourinho taking his final bow as Chelsea manager as his side put up an unbelievably feeble defence of the League Title they had won 12 months earlier, the supporters can be forgiven for thinking Conte's would be a rebuilding job initially. However, after a good start to the campaign was suddenly tempered by defeats at home by Liverpool and away to Arsenal, the new manager's credentials were quickly called into question. His response, initiated mid-game at the Emirates Stadium as a damage-limitation exercise, was to switch to a back three with Victor Moses and Marcos Alonso employed as galloping wing-backs. The impact was immediate, and Chelsea embarked on a 13-match winning run in the League. After the last of those victories, a 4-2 triumph over Stoke City on New Year's Eve, Conte's rejuvenated team ended the year six points clear of Liverpool at the top of the table. However, it was a game almost two months earlier which gets included in this book for one simple reason: It was the best performance I can recall seeing from any Chelsea side, throughout my entire first fifty years of supporting them.

Remember, remember the 5th November. Well, Everton's grossly-overrated centre-half Ashley Williams will have nightmares for years to come when he recalls Bonfire Night 2016. I'd never rated Williams, and in truth never much liked him after he stirred the pot in the wake of Eden Hazard's sending-off for trying to retrieve the ball from a fat 17-year-old ball 'boy' at Swansea, where Williams was captain, in 2013. How Williams ever got the Toffees gig is beyond me, he was the ultimate plodder, a man for whom the phrase "I've seen milk turn quicker" might have been invented, and he was at his right level at Swansea. Particularly when they were in the second-flight.

On the night in question, as Chelsea rinsed Everton by five goals to nil, and barely got out of first gear once the fifth had been notched, it was a joy to watch Diego Costa match Williams' only attributes – his CV says 'I'm a big man and I'm very strong' – and Hazard pull him all over the pitch in a masterclass that exploited all of the Welshman's many limitations. I'd love to think it was Hazard's way of avenging Williams for his comments after the ball boy incident.

Once Chelsea's Belgian genius opened the scoring in the 19th minute and Alonso doubled it just seconds later, the game turned into a procession. The level of Chelsea's passing, the swiftness of movement, and the elegance of the entire performance was breathtaking. Costa made it three before the break, before Hazard again, and Pedro completed the scoring. Hazard's footprints were all over the performance, he was mesmerising, but the little Spaniard Pedro wasn't far behind. He flitted about like a wasp, almost impossible for Everton's players to catch, and he was instrumental in so many of the flowing moves which caught the eye that day, and got me thinking that it was the best ninety minutes I'd seen.

As I left the ground with Sam, I told him to remember and cherish that performance and the fact he'd been at the game to witness it. It might be a while before it's bettered.

SUNDAY 21ST MAY 2017

Premier League
Chelsea 5 Sunderland 1

The weekend of 20th and 21st May 2017 was one of the best I'll ever have, as a number of important events all came together, culminating in the first game I was ever able to attend with both my boys. That Chelsea would be handed the Premier League trophy that day, with Eddie McCreadie inside the ground at the time, made the day nigh on perfect.

Five of us – Mark Worrall, Mark Meehan, David Johnstone, Neil Smith and I – had been working for a year or so on writing a book about McCreadie and his boys of 1977, the primarily home-grown squad of youngsters who achieved promotion against a backdrop of financial turbulence, transfer embargoes and a voluntary pay cut that each of those players signed up to. We had also been working closely with the club to put on a tribute night to that team. Perhaps the thing we'd worked hardest on was persuading McCreadie to attend, but our former Scottish defender and manager was famously nervous about flying, and had therefore not returned to these shores since he'd left them almost forty years earlier. Eddie was a fantastic subject matter and a lovely man, but he was adamant that he wouldn't be coming over for a night in his honour.

I'm somewhat biased but I liked the Eddie Mac book. Mark Meehan did an incredible job of hunting down all the players from that era, only one of whom chose to have no part in it. One other, Peter Bonetti, was sadly too unwell to contribute and has since passed away. Ray Wilkins gave a fantastic interview and was something of a driving force in getting the tribute night agreed, even though he was unable to attend. He wanted to ensure that all his former teammates got the tributes and recognition they deserved.

Neil and David contributed a superb chapter about their travels around the country as part of Eddie McCreadie's Blue and White Army, and Mark Worrall and I added a few bits of our own and broadly concentrated on reminding readers of a period in time that neither Mark nor I actually look old enough to have lived through.

I have to say, Chelsea Football Club were incredibly supportive of our efforts, particularly in regard to the tribute night. They were very generous when negotiating a price for us to book Under the Bridge – the nightclub situated underneath Stamford Bridge's East Stand – and freed up a number of hotel rooms for ex-players and staff attending. When Roman Abramovich discovered that we were struggling to break even, he personally covered the losses. When Chelsea played at home to Crystal Palace on 1st April, a full-page advert for the tribute night appeared in the matchday programme, free of charge. I'm not slow to criticise our Board at times, but they get it right more often than they get it wrong, and I wouldn't want anybody else running our great club.

Chelsea surprisingly lost the aforementioned clash with Crystal Palace, but were already well on their way to winning their fifth Premier League title. It duly arrived when Michy Batshuyai scored a late winner to beat West Bromwich Albion at The Hawthorns. Chelsea had two games remaining, at home to Watford the following Monday, and at home again to Sunderland six days later. The trophy would be presented after that game. The tribute night to Eddie McCreadie and his team would be held the night before. And as if a title-winning weekend isn't good enough, I then received a voice message forwarded to me by David Johnstone. It was from Eddie McCreadie, apologising profusely for messing us around but asking if he could please attend the night at Under the Bridge after all. He and his partner, Linda, had discussed it and felt that it was too good an opportunity to miss. My heart jumped and I suspect my co-writers all had similar emotions.

All tickets had been sold at this stage, and our publicity had been amended to clarify that Eddie would not be attending. We needed to ensure there was no ambiguity around this. My immediate, impetuous response to Eddie's message was to let everybody know about the change of plan, but David quite rightly said it would be better to say nothing until we knew Eddie and Linda were on the plane. There was still potential for Eddie to rethink his decision, and we were therefore better advised to keep it under our hat until we had absolute certainty he was on his way.

Eddie and Linda landed at Heathrow on the Friday morning, the day before the tribute event would take place. Eddie's assistant during his time as Chelsea manager, Ken Shellito, flew in from Malaysia around the same time. We didn't know it at the time, but in flying Ken over to London we gave him a last opportunity to meet with Eddie, their boys of 77, and a number of his former teammates such as Bobby Tambling and John Hollins before the Sunderland game on the Sunday. Sadly, Ken passed away less than two years later.

With Eddie and Ken in London, we knew we had pulled off a coup.

Numerous players from their time in charge were certain to attend, and others such as Mickey Thomas, Kerry Dixon and Nigel Spackman were coming along to support the event. And with the help of friendly journalists Henry Winter and Andy Lines, we had some great publicity given to both the book and the event in The Guardian and Daily Mirror respectively.

The night itself went off without a hitch. The feedback we received, and continue to receive, suggests that all who attended had a great time. From a personal perspective, I was so happy to have my dad there, and I have a great photo of him with Eddie that I will always cherish. My dad took me to so many games when Eddie was a player, and then throughout his time as manager, and it made me truly happy that we were able to be together that night. Daniel also came, while Sam was otherwise engaged. However, the following day and for the first time ever, I sat flanked by my two sons in the Shed Upper as Chelsea beat Sunderland 5-1, prior to lifting the Premier League trophy at the end of the game. Forty years earlier I had been at Stamford Bridge for that last game of the season against Hull, which was also a wild celebration. That day Eddie took to the pitch and gave a speech. Forty years later it was the turn of Antonio Conte and the departing John Terry. On both occasions the Bridge crackled with emotion, as did I. Truly, days I'll remember all my life.

As a footnote to the above, when Eddie and Linda returned Stateside they took the trouble to write a note to each of us to thank us for our efforts, and to say how touched they were to receive such warmth from everybody present. It was clear that Eddie had no idea of the strength of feeling the supporters of that time have for him. That note means a lot to me and, much like the photo of Eddie with my dad, I will treasure it forever.

SATURDAY 9TH FEBRUARY 2019

Conference Premier

Wrexham 1 Dagenham & Redbridge 0

When Mickey Thomas was making the most of a stellar career, he was always a bundle of energy with a sweet left-foot, a tenacity and will to win unmatched by most, and a smile never far away from his face. I made the point in *Celery*, before I knew him personally, that Mickey was a player I always thought was made for Chelsea Football Club and its supporters. I was over the moon when he joined in 1984.

Since getting to know Mickey and, as with Joey Jones, him becoming somebody I consider to be a close friend now, I have learned that the happy-go-lucky footballer who we quickly fell in love with at the Bridge, retains the same lust for life and fantastic sense of humour that he had during his playing days. I love chatting to him and catching up in person when we can. He's still a bundle of energy, still always on the go. Like Joey, Mickey is enormously popular within the game and amongst the fans of the clubs he played for, plus many supporters of other clubs who just respect the man for his talent and personality. For many older supporters, he's a throwback to a bygone, golden era. The maverick era.

When Mickey told me he had been feeling unwell and was having trouble digesting food, I suspected he had some kind of blockage that needed clearing. I'm fairly clueless when it comes to medical matters, but fortunately some of Mickey's other friends are more clued up. It was former England and Manchester United captain Bryan Robson, a close friend of Mickey's, who identified that this was cause for concern and told Mickey to get himself seen by a doctor urgently. Mickey was referred to hospital and the issue was identified as cancer of the oesophagus. When he told me the diagnosis I was stunned, and felt a little guilty for not realising it might be something this serious. Mickey often makes comments about me being intelligent, but I'm not, and this may have proven it.

Mickey was booked in to start chemotherapy treatment on 11th February 2019, and he was understandably frightened by the prospect of this and his situation generally. The story broke in the press a few days earlier, the day before I had arranged to go up to Wrexham to see him and Joey. Joey has his own health problems. He had life-saving heart surgery in 2002 and now, almost twenty years on, has chronic heart failure and with the help of his local hospital manages his irreparable condition as best he can.

On the day I went up to visit, Wrexham were playing at home to Dagenham and Redbridge. Given that I live in Redbridge, I should probably have been supporting the visitors, but it's Wrexham who I want to see do well. I don't do second teams as such, for me it's Chelsea and no-one else, but I've long since had a soft spot for the North Wales club as they were the club which provided three key members of that great 1983/84 promotion team – Joey , Mickey and Eddie Niedzwiecki – plus the very man that Johnny Neal's Blue and White Army was named after. Four Chelsea greats, and four really good men. When I once told John Neal how friendly and approachable I had found his three former charges from their youngest days at the Racecourse Ground, he beamed with pride and said "Aye, well they had a good upbringing." And when I go to Wrexham, I see clear evidence of a friendly club with its feet firmly on the ground, that deserves a reversal of the fortune which has seen them drop out of the English Football League in recent years. As for Dagenham and Redbridge, they were managed at the time by Peter Taylor, a former Spurs man, so they were the enemy regardless of where I live.

When Mickey arrived at the ground he was on the phone to John Hartson, one of many ex-pros who had called to wish him well. He had received personal messages from a number of his former Chelsea team-mates, including Colin Lee, Pat Nevin and Robert Isaac. John Bumstead and Colin Pates had asked me to pass on their best wishes to him. If ever I needed proof of just how popular Mickey is within the football world, this was it. He had no enemies, only friends. I actually felt quite emotional already, and when the Wrexham supporters began singing "There's only one Mickey Thomas" early in the game, I had a lump in my throat. And then I remembered me and six thousand others singing the same thing at Hillsborough when he sparked out Andy Blair and the ref didn't see it, and that cheered me up a bit.

Wrexham won that day but Mickey was clearly not right, and he left around half-time. I stopped over that night at Joey's niece's very nice pub/bed and breakfast on the outskirts of Wrexham, and Joey and his wife Janice came over for dinner that evening. I was glad I got to see Mickey before his chemo started, although he was understandably a little more subdued than normal. He called me from the hospital on the Monday morning and I was glad he did that, even though I knew there were no words I could utter that would make him any less frightened, so I just reminded him of how strong he is and always has been – this is a man who Roy Keane once complimented on his physique, long after his playing days were over – and emphasised that he literally had the support of thousands as he fought this battle.

Turn the clock forward six months and my son, Daniel, and I are Mickey's guests in the box that he hosts at Old Trafford. A really nice lady by the name of Debbie Goward runs DHL's contract with Manchester United, and she has always looked after and been a good friend to Mickey. Mickey himself has just come through the other end of his treatment and although still a little frail, looks better than I expected him to. Daniel had spent some time with Mickey and I in London's Landmark Hotel before the 2018 FA Cup Final between Chelsea and United, and really enjoyed meeting him at last, having heard so many stories about him from me.

The game at Old Trafford didn't go Chelsea's way, United winning by a somewhat-flattering 4-0 scoreline in what was Frank Lampard's first game in charge of the Blues. But for once, the football wasn't the main event that day. Neither was the celebrity hob-nobbing (although I did sit down with Andy Ritchie and get the inside track on why he turned down a move to Chelsea in 1980). This was a good day, a happy day. Mickey Thomas was back at the wheel, smiling and greeting visitors, amongst friends and recovering, if not yet fully recovered, from the biggest challenge of his life.

MONDAY 8TH APRIL 2019

Premier League

Chelsea 2 West Ham United 0

The next chapter feels particularly self-indulgent, but it figures for a reason. It might just feature a moment where my life peaked, and Chelsea Football Club – Eden Hazard in particular – played a significant part.

Lisa had long held a dream to spend our 25th anniversary in an over-water villa in The Maldives. I think she probably first mentioned this at our wedding in 1994, knowing it would take 25 years to pay for it. However, thanks to some serious saving and a cracking deal in the Virgin Holidays winter sale, we were able to make her dream come true. We booked nine days in a resort called Finolhu, on the Baa Atoll. Lisa did all the research and assured me she had found the perfect resort for us. I personally would have preferred to run around New York or another US city, and was unconvinced that the Indian Ocean and I would actually get on. How wrong I was.

Due to Lisa's job in a school, we have to take our holidays outside of term time. Conscious of the fact that our summer coincides with The Maldives' rainy season, we booked our trip to take place in April, during the Easter break. It would mean I had to miss West Ham's visit to the Bridge, which was a Monday evening game.

To be honest, we'd only been in Finolhu five minutes before it dawned on me that we might just have landed in paradise. The sun was shining brightly when our seaplane landed, but was starting to go down over the ocean and the water villas by the time we completed our check-in. We'd been travelling for 13 hours but the sight of that sunset quickly erased any tiredness we were feeling, as did the first view of our villa with its huge wooden patio and steps directly into the sea. I grew up on caravan holidays in Norfolk and Devon, fantastic times but quite different to this.

Another thing that was quite different for us was the time difference, and how it was calculated. Obviously there is a time difference between London and Norfolk – roughly about thirty years – but Finolhu is the only place I know that decides its own time. The Maldives are generally six hours ahead of UK time, but the Finolhu resort puts the clock forward an extra hour to give its visitors an additional sixty minutes of sunshine. It also means that 8pm kick-offs in London start at 3am in Finolhu, which feels a lot later than 2am elsewhere in paradise. And to make life just that little bit harder, Chelsea were playing again three nights later, against Slavia Prague in the Europa League.

Maurizio Sarri's season in charge of Chelsea was divisive to say the least. Not quite as reviled amongst the supporters as Rafael Benitez, but certainly not as popular as most of the other 273 (approximately) managers who have been in and out of SW6's revolving over the past thirty years, Sarri's year at the helm was characterised by dull performances, drab tactics and the occasional hammering. It also included a Europa League win – with a thrashing dished out to once-mighty Arsenal in the Final – and a top-three finish, so I'm fairly ambivalent to Sarri and what he brought to the club. However, I do believe Eden Hazard largely carried the team throughout that campaign.

On the night of the West Ham game, while Lisa was fast asleep beside me, Hazard once again illuminated Stamford Bridge. He is the best player I have ever seen at Chelsea, and only Ruud Gullit really comes close. He's not my favourite, that will always be Joey (without Joey joining during that horrible 1982/83 season, we probably would never have seen the likes of Hazard and Gullit at the Bridge) but Hazard did things with a football in a Chelsea shirt that no others were capable of repeating, certainly not with the same regularity.

Chelsea beat West Ham 2-0 that night, and I managed to somehow stay awake until 5am watching it. Old, but still a maverick. Hazard scored both goals, and for the first he literally slalomed through the Hammers' entire back line before sweeping the ball home. How I didn't disturb not just Lisa but the whole of Finolhu is beyond me, because I was dancing on water, literally, when that goal went in. Dancing on water in paradise, with the love of my life sleeping next to me, midway through the holiday she'd always dreamed of and had definitely earned over the years. I felt like a very lucky boy that night, everything seemed perfect.

I didn't even bother trying to stay up again for the Slavia Prague game three nights later. A maverick, but still old.

PRESS BOXES, PRESS CONFERENCES, CONCERTS AND MORE

Writing *Celery!* and getting to know so many interesting people on the strength of it, has brought me into contact with a lot of people I wouldn't have otherwise met, and into situations I would never have previously dreamed of. As a kid growing up, my latter school years coincided with the ska and Two Tone craze, and Madness were one of my favourite bands. Over the years I have seen them live on numerous occasions, but in the summer of 2009 I saw them from an angle and a distance I had never thought possible.

I went to the Madness gig at Victoria Park, Bow with David Johnstone and a couple of his friends who worked in Chelsea's security team. Our friend, Graham Bush, was their regular bass player at the time, but their original bassist, Mark Bedford, played at this gig. I did have the pleasure of seeing Graham play with them three years later in Brighton, the blue lights on his instrument a tribute to his and our team. On this particular night Graham was backstage amongst other friends and family members of the band, but imagine his surprise when he looked to the side of the stage and saw David and I singing and dancing, literally sharing a stage with the Nutty Boys. David, as always, knew somebody, and that somebody allowed us to have that prime viewing spot throughout the duration of the concert. Truth be told, after initially, very excitedly watching the standard crowd eruption as Madness kicked off their gig with the heavy heavy monster sound of the iconic One Step Beyond, I did get a bit carried away, and I must have spent the first 15 minutes of the concert sending multiple texts from side stage, with smug 'wish you were here?' type captions to various friends and family members.

Another funny moment courtesy of David came one Saturday evening when I had just got home from Chelsea. My phone rang and it was David, who just said "I'm with somebody who wants to speak to you." The next thing I knew, I was chatting to Dougie Trendle – Buster Bloodvessel from Bad Manners – who I would meet soon after when he and his band played a gig at Oxford Street's 100 Club to celebrate well-known Chelsea fan and criminal barrister supreme, Mark Wyeth, becoming a Queen's Counsel. During a difficult period when I lost my job and my then-employer were trying to take the proverbial, Mark was a great help in setting me up with a top-notch employment barrister friend of his, who very quickly helped me give them an embarrassing bloody nose.

Guys like David and Mark were invaluable to me around that time, as was Mark Worrall. Joey Jones and Mickey Thomas also rallied round, and they really kept my spirits up at a time when I felt under severe pressure and hit some pretty dark places.

Trips to football matches and associated events have always been a lot of fun. I first went up to Wrexham to see Joey with two friends, Peter Ground and Mark Brown, when the Welsh side were still in the Football League. On a freezing January day, the three of us drove up to the Racecourse Ground for a clash with Hartlepool United. Joey was joint-manager at the time, and took us into the home dressing room as he was giving a pre-match team talk He told the players that we had travelled up from London to watch them, and to not less us down. The three of us just smiled enigmatically. It was a great day, although we joked that we should have stuck the half-time pasties down our trousers to keep us warm.

After the game, Joey was talking to a journalist from the local paper and mentioned that Peter, Mark and I had travelled up from London for the game. He asked if he could interview one of us, and a few days later Joey sent me the newspaper cutting which quoted me as saying I thought Wrexham had played well in the second half, particularly young substitute Matty Done, who brought them level after the visitors had controlled the first half. It also referred to the three of us as Chelsea supporters, which was fine with Mark and I, but less acceptable to West Ham season-ticket holder Peter.

The trips up to Wrexham have all been really enjoyable, but too infrequent if I'm honest. One of the times we went up was for a game against Torquay, and for obvious reasons it was nice to see Colin Lee and Joey alongside each other again, albeit with no cocky winger around to put the fear of God into.

Mickey Thomas' main source of income nowadays comes through work with Manchester United, for whom he is a club ambassador. He is a corporate host at Old Trafford on match days, and travels to European away games and other big matches and events. We've met up a couple of times in recent seasons when United have been playing at Wembley, and the club representatives have been staying in the Landmark Hotel in Marylebone. On one occasion, Stoke City were also staying there ahead of a game at Spurs, and I was able to catch up with their then-coach Eddie Niedzwiecki too. Eddie remains close friends with Joey and Mickey.

Mickey enjoys visits to London, and during his time working in radio we went to a number of games together when he was down in the Capital. I recall one game when United were playing at Arsenal, and he got me into the press room and the press box. The facilities were superb and the catering for the media was outstanding. This was during my 25-year portly phase, and I remember having a full meal before kick-off, followed by fish and chips at half-time. And it was all free. I also remember walking down the steps of the press box at half-time and somebody tapping my right shoulder as they ran past me on the left. As I looked down at the person speeding past me, I saw former Gunners full-back Lee Dixon look at me with a huge grin and say "Race ya" before disappearing. I just stood there laughing at the surreal nature of what had just happened!

On two occasions, both at Stamford Bridge, Mickey took me into post-match press conferences. Both were during Chelsea's double-winning 2009/10 campaign. One was following an FA Cup tie when the Blues beat Cardiff City 4-1. Manager Carlo Ancelotti seemed happy with the outcome, but I remember visiting manager Dave Jones getting very snarky with a Welsh local reporter who criticised his tactics. I reckon there was a bit of history between them that I wasn't aware of.

After that presser, Mickey and I were on our way out of the ground when we bumped into Chelsea steward Frank Steer. Frank and Mickey know each other from right back to Mickey's playing days at Chelsea. He offered us a lift, but as we tried to leave we discovered that the gates to Stamford Bridge were locked and nobody was allowed to leave. World War III had broken out on the King's Road between rival fans, and all surrounding streets were being cleared. A tanned but somewhat bemused Charlie Cooke was also locked in that day.

The other press conference I attended – and this really was my favourite – came after Chelsea had beaten Liverpool 2-0 in October. The Reds were deep into their 30-year search for the domestic league title and had been right in the mix the season before, but had made a disappointing start to this campaign, with manager Rafael Benitez starting to show clear signs of frustration with his team and his lot on Merseyside. One particular journalist, the late Ian McGarry, who I believe was writing for the Daily Mail at the time, had Benitez on a string during that session, really getting under the Spaniard's skin with his line of questioning. It was a joy to see. To make matters funnier, you could see that the more Benitez became rattled, the more McGarry turned the screw. I whispered to Mickey "What would happen now if I put my hand up, announced myself as Kelvin Barker from CFCUK fanzine, and asked 'Mr Benitez, why do you always blame everybody else when your team loses?'" Mickey laughed and said I should find out, but as much as I would have loved to have done just that, I'm not sure it would have done Mickey any favours if his guest had pulled such a stunt. And anyway, McGarry was doing just fine as it was.

HERE'S TO THE NEXT FIFTY

Let's get one thing straight here – my aim is to support Chelsea for one hundred years, so I'm only halfway there at the moment. The second volume of *Days* will be written and published around 2071, so make a note in your diary. It's off to a good start already, because six months into my second half-century, the mighty Blues went and won the Champions League again. The pandemic and restricted ticket allocations ensured I wouldn't make it to my third Final, and I actually ended up watching it in a hotel in Dorchester, on what was Lisa's birthday. 29th May is a lucky day for me, but also a good one for Chelsea as it was also the date on which we battered Arsenal in Baku to lift the 2019 Europa League trophy. Who knows what the content of Days Part Two might comprise? But that's for us to worry about when I'm 105.

What I wanted to do with *this* book was to show how Chelsea Football Club has been a constant companion to me throughout the last fifty years; not just on match days, but in my day-to-day and personal lives too. It's not been the only constant – my parents, brother and two pals, Patrick and Simon, have gone the distance too – but it's a fairly exclusive club.

Some of the chapters and the memories they invoke are more generic than others, they don't necessarily tie in to anything more specific than the fact that they made a particular period in my life a really happy one (August 1983 to May 1985) or they gave me as much pleasure for ninety minutes (5-0 v Everton in November 2016) as I do Lisa occasionally. That's also usually two lots of 45 minutes with a 15-minute break in the middle. There's rarely an extra-time period these days, not at our age. But there's an increasing amount of injury-time being added on.

There were undoubtedly times during my childhood when it felt like the mighty Blues were the single most important companion I had. I put Chelsea above all others, and they continually let me down. But like a smitten teenager, I kept on going back for more. Every weekend and often in midweek too, I would put it on a plate for them and they would just take advantage and then leave me disappointed. They were fluttering their eyelids at a slutty piece called Division Three, but I was too besotted to realise. Thankfully, the 'Boys in Blue in Division Two' eventually got their act together in that very special summer of 1983, and despite a few small bumps in the road since, we've generally had a lovely time together over the past four decades. I'll never forget the climax they gave me one Saturday night in Munich when it was so good there were literally fireworks.

Maturity came late to me - and I've tried to ignore it ever since it showed its ugly head, truth be known – but it has, sort of, in a small way, despite all my best efforts to resist, eventually crept in and put its feet under my table. As a result, *Days* has incorporated all the really important things: births, deaths and marriages – one of which is still going strong. The births involve my sons, but with Poppy being born outside of the football season, a Chelsea link was less obvious. But there is one. Of course there is one. On the afternoon of Sunday 11th June 1995, while Lisa was in labour preparing to deliver my only daughter, England were getting beaten at Wembley by Brazil. The score was 3-1, the England goalscorer Graeme Le Saux. He was ex-Chelsea at the time, but a link is nevertheless established.

More than anything, what I wanted this book to be is a love letter. A love letter to my wife, my three children and grandson, my parents, my siblings, my wider family and my friends, including those mentioned within these pages who came into my life and enriched it all too briefly, and will never get the chance to read about it. I love you all. It's also a love letter to my childhood, to Shepherds Bush (but, I repeat, not its football club), to innocence and to myriad happy memories. And, of course, it's a love letter to Chelsea Football Club, my constant companion for more than half a century.

Over the past fifty years as they've ridden pillion alongside me, Chelsea have introduced joy, pain, pleasure, anger, ecstasy and frustration into my life. I've often described them as a soap opera or an accident waiting to happen, yet as I write this concluding chapter on Sunday 13th February 2022, forty years to the day that a mid-table Division Two Blues side caused a sensation by knocking European Champions Liverpool out of the FA Cup, I'm doing so with the broadest of smiles on my face. You see, yesterday Chelsea beat Brazilian side Palmeiras in the Final of the FIFA Club World Cup in Abu Dhabi. They are officially the greatest club on planet earth. Literally the best team in the world. Who'd have thought it? Cheers Dad, it didn't work out too bad in the end.

Come on you mighty Blues.

Kelvin Barker,

DAYS (I'LL REMEMBER ALL MY LIFE)

The morning after the night before,
February 2022.

Thank you for the days,
Those endless days, those sacred days you gave me.
I'm thinking of the days, I won't forget a single day, believe me.
I bless the light, I bless the light that lights on you, believe me,
And though you're gone, you're with me every single day, believe me.
Days I'll remember all my life.

(Writer: Ray Davies)

EPILOGUE

It could only happen at Chelsea.

Two weeks after I dotted the last 'i' and crossed the last 't' on this book, Russia invaded Ukraine and the world became a significantly darker place. Roman Abramovich's long-mooted, supposed friendship with Vladimir Putin became a focus of many politicians and journalists, and Abramovich announced he would be selling Chelsea Football Club. Soon after, the Conservative government imposed sanctions on our Russian owner, leaving the future of the club in turmoil. Thankfully, as I write this, a new ownership is being sworn in and Todd Boehly's Blue and White Army will soon march for the first time. I will march with them from 2022/23 and as long as my body allows.

As Abramovich was such a generous benefactor of the club, it perhaps should be assumed that the glorious triumphs of the past two decades *might* not be repeated any time soon. I'll leave the speculation and conjecture to others, because I have no idea of the strength or otherwise of Abramovich's relationship with Putin. Instead, if this does prove to be the case I'll simply quote Doctor Seuss:

"Don't cry because it's over, smile because it happened."

Thank you, Roman Abramovich, for what you gave to Chelsea Football Club. I'll take the memories of your tenure to the grave with me.

As is evidenced by some of the stories in this book, I've known some pretty bleak times as a Chelsea supporter. The relegations, the humiliating Cup giant-killing defeats, the ridiculous and often rapid transformations of Blues teams from successful to woeful, and the misfortune and mismanagement which has at times left the club on the brink of financial ruin – I've seen them all, although never previously at a time when Chelsea held the titles of both European and World champions!

We now move on to another new era, to making more memories and to, hopefully, continuing the successes of the past 25 years through the next quarter of a century and beyond. If we don't achieve them, we'll still be Chelsea. If we do, we'll still be massive.

GATE 17
THE COMPLETE COLLECTION
(SUMMER 2022)

CHELSEA

Over Land and Sea – Mark Worrall
Chelsea here, Chelsea There – Kelvin Barker, David Johnstone, Mark Worrall
Chelsea Football Fanzine – the best of cfcuk
One Man Went to Mow – Mark Worrall
Making History Not Reliving It –
Kelvin Barker, David Johnstone, Mark Worrall
Celery! Representing Chelsea in the 1980s – Kelvin Barker
Stuck On You, a year in the life of a Chelsea supporter – Walter Otton
Palpable Discord, a year of drama and dissent at Chelsea – Clayton Beerman
Rhyme and Treason – Carol Ann Wood
Eddie Mac Eddie Mac – Eddie McCreadie's Blue & White Army
The Italian Job, A Chelsea thriller starring Antonio Conte – Mark Worrall
Carefree! Chelsea Chants & Terrace Culture – Mark Worrall, Walter Otton
Diamonds, Dynamos and Devils – Tim Rolls
Arrivederci Antonio, The Italian Job (part two) – Mark Worrall
Where Were You When We Were Shocking? – Neil L. Smith
Chelsea, 100 Memorable Matches – Chelsea Chadder
Bewitched, Bothered & Bewildered – Carol Ann Wood
Stamford Bridge Is Falling Down – Tim Rolls
Cult Fiction – Dean Mears
Chelsea, If Twitter Was Around When… – Chelsea Chadder
Blue Army – Vince Cooper
Liquidator 1969-70 A Chelsea Memoir – Mark Worrall
When Skies Are Grey, Super Frank, Chelsea And The Coronavirus Crisis – Mark Worrall
Tales Of The (Chelsea) Unexpected – David Johnstone & Neil L Smith
The Ultimate Unofficial Chelsea Quiz Book – Chelsea Chadder
Blue Days – Chris Wright
Let The Celery Decide – Walter Otton
Blue Hitmen – Paul Radcliffe
Sexton For God – Tim Rolls
Tales From The Shed – Edited by Mark Worrall
For Better Or Worse – Jason Gibbins
Come Along And Sing This Song – Johnny Neal's Blue And White Army
Days (I'll Remember All My Life) – Kelvin Barker
Imagine Not Being Chelsea – Chris Wright

FICTION

Blue Murder, Chelsea Till I Die – Mark Worrall
The Wrong Outfit – Al Gregg
The Red Hand Gang – Walter Otton
Coming Clean – Christopher Morgan
This Damnation – Mark Worrall
Poppy – Walter Otton

NON FICTION

Roe2Ro – Walter Otton
Shorts – Walter Otton
England International Football Team Quiz & Trivia Book – George Cross

www.gate17books.co.uk

Printed in Great Britain
by Amazon